CALLED TO GREATNESS

31 DEVOTIONS TO IGNITE THE FAITH OF FATHERS & SONS

DAN BRITTON
& JIMMY PAGE

BroadStreet
PUBLISHING

Published by BroadStreet Publishing Group, LLC
Racine, Wisconsin, USA
www.broadstreetpublishing.com

CALLED TO GREATNESS
31 DEVOTIONS TO IGNITE THE FAITH OF FATHERS & SONS

Stock or custom editions of BroadStreet Publishing titles may be purchased in bulk for
educational, business, ministry, fundraising, or sales promotional use. For information, please e-mail info@broadstreetpublishing.com.

Cover design by Chris Garborg at www.garborgdesign.com
Interior by Katherine Lloyd at www.theDESKonline.com
Author photos © 2010 by Dan Michael Hodges

Printed in China

8/15–1

This book is dedicated to our sons
who have all responded
to God's Call to Greatness.

Elijah Britton

Jimmy Page

Jacob Page

John Page

With much love.

Table of Contents

Introduction

*T*he relationship between a father and son is one of the most anointed relationships ever designed by God. In fact, it existed before the creation of the world, as seen in the very nature of God—Father, Son, and Holy Spirit. When Jesus left the heavens and became a man, the Father was overjoyed. We see evidence of this when Jesus emerges from the water of baptism and hears the voice of His Father, in Matthew 3:16–17 HCSB:

> After Jesus was baptized, He went up immediately from the water. The heavens suddenly opened for Him, and He saw the Spirit of God descending like a dove and coming down on Him. And there came a voice from heaven: This is My beloved Son. I take delight in Him!

God's favor rests on His Son, Jesus. In the same way, God's favor and delight rests upon us. When we discover that we are God's beloved, we need to embrace it—at which point we can become His beloved to others. Fathers, have you embraced God's words about how valuable you are to Him? Do you feel His pleasure and affection? Once you do, you are empowered to become the beloved to your son.

The Father's statement "My beloved Son" is more than just an approval or validation. It is a manifestation of pure and true love. It's a statement of identity. Your son is your beloved; that simply means precious, adored, cherished, treasured, prized, highly regarded, admired, esteemed, and favorite one. Unfortunately, most sons don't experience this and instead feel they are no good, forgotten, worthless, rejected, and unlovable. No matter what they do, they do not measure up to their father's expectations. But this is not God's design for this relationship.

Can you imagine if every son knew that he was his father's beloved? It would be life-changing because it would eliminate the son's quest to earn his father's love and acceptance. It would end the performance-based relationship that is dependent on how well he does on the field, in the classroom, in his career, or on stage. His identity and place in the family would be secure and not affected by circumstances, successes, or failures. Sons would live with security, confidence, and courage knowing that their dad will always be there for them.

But it doesn't stop there. God the Father tops it off with "I delight in Him." The Father is thrilled, overjoyed, and pleased with His Son. Every son needs and deserves to hear these five words from his father: *I am pleased with you.* God can do much with these five words.

As fathers, we desire to experience this type of love with our sons. The Bible has given us countless examples of the father–son relationship by:

- Fathers blessing their sons
- Fathers modeling their walk with God for their sons
- Fathers mentoring their sons
- Fathers asking God to heal their sons
- Fathers reconciling broken and damaged relationships with their sons
- Fathers waiting for their wayward sons to come back home

Called to Greatness is a powerful tool to ignite the faith of fathers and sons by intentionally bringing them together every day for thirty-one days. In one month, God can do miraculous things to develop, repair, and mature your relationship. This book is best utilized if you decide to commit one month to fire up your relationship and go through these thirty-one devotionals together.

It would be beneficial to define the health of your relationship before you begin. Knowing where you are will help you know where you want to go. It also gives you insight into how to approach the relationship. Most likely, you could define your relationship in one of three ways:

1. **Hot** –You are engaged, encouraged, and enthusiastic. You feel very good about your father–son relationship. You would give it a rating of 8 or above on a 1-to-10 scale. Both of you would say it is close-knit, solid, and healthy. You spend time together and have a strong connection and bond. This devotional will be extremely helpful in continuing to strengthen what you already have. Don't let up. Keep it strong by investing in it with this devotional. Take it to the next level. Never be content with where you are. There is always room for improvement.

2. **Warm** –You may be so-so, stuck, or stable. You would rate your relationship 5 to 7 out of 10. There is some intentionality, but distractions and busyness get in the way of it being great. Maybe yours is better than many relationships around you, but you aren't experiencing the fullness that you know you could. You are at a critical time to fuel the fire and allow these thirty-one days to be the igniter you need. Give everything you have to repair needed areas and grow your relationship.

3. **Cold** –You are distant, disengaged, or damaged. Your relationship may be marked by conflict, disappointment, or even anger. You would rate your relationship 4 or below. There are real and hard reasons why it's cold. This book could be the very thing that breathes new life into your relationship. Ask God for a fresh touch to reconcile and restore the relationship to where God wants it. Believe in Him to do a mighty work.

It really doesn't matter how you rate your relationship right now; that simply gives you a starting point for discussion and improvement. It's never how you start, but how you finish, that counts. Enter the process with a spirit of humility and courage.

In today's world, it is rare to find the traditional father–son relationship. No matter what situation you find yourself in, it's important to overcome any obstacles or barriers and decide to cultivate the relationship and let God do His work. Even if you don't have a father, pursue and ask a father figure to walk with you for thirty-one days.

Noted sociologist Dr. David Popenoe says, "Involved fathers bring positive benefits to their children that no other person is as likely to bring." *Called to Greatness* provides fathers and sons devotional readings around themes like loving unconditionally, walking in integrity, pursuing purity, making a difference, living a life of significance, and being great in the eyes of God. *Called to Greatness* invites and empowers fathers and sons to become great men who humbly and faithfully serve a great God.

With these thirty-one devotions, fathers can maximize their time with their sons with just ten minutes each day for an entire month. Each devotional features a life-application story,

Scripture, application questions, a Take Action section for discussion and journaling, and a heart- and mind-transforming prayer.

Carve out the time. Decide that your relationship with your son (or father) deserves thirty-one days of focus. This could be one of the most significant things you do with him. Don't delay. Start today and let God begin to do His work.

Called to Greatness may have the only introduction that makes you do some work before you dive into the book. Everything that's important in life is worth the effort to make it great. As we shared, each session ends with a Take Action section and a prayer. We would like for you to start now and assess your relationship to make sure you're on the same page before diving in. It's vital to define and manage expectations. Getting both of you on the same page will allow the Spirit of the Living God to do His work. The Spirit of the Lord shows up powerfully in unity! Get connected. Get unified.

Here we go!

Dan Britton & Jimmy Page

TAKE ACTION

1. Establish your starting point.

Individually rate your relationship from 1 to 10 with 10 being the best. Share your number with each other. With no criticism or complaint, share why you gave it that rating. Be honest and transparent with each other.

Write your starting point number here: _____

2. Discuss your relational temperature.

Based on your scores, would your relationship be considered hot, warm, or cold? Go back and look at the descriptions of each category. Would you agree or change the description of your relationship? Talk openly with each other about your assessment.

Write your relationship temperature here: _____

3. Create a vision for the future.

Discuss what you're expecting from the next thirty-one days as you go through the process of investing in your relationship. Take a look into the future and describe what you hope your relationship will look like at the end of the thirty-one days. Write down that picture in words here. Ask and trust God for that.

Describe your expectations for your relationship here:

Take the
Called to
Greatness
31-Day Challenge

It's time to take the Called to Greatness 31-Day Challenge together as father and son. We expect this 31-day journey together to ignite our faith and strengthen our relationship as it prepares us for a life of purpose, passion, and power.

Lord Jesus, we are responding to the call to greatness placed on our lives. We want to be transformed more and more into Your likeness and be connected to each other for Your purposes. We expect You, Lord, to do the miraculous in us and through us along this journey together. We ask for Your help in order to have the relationship You've designed and desire us to have. Amen.

On this day, we take the Called to Greatness 31-Day Challenge:

_____   _____

Father's Signature   Date

_____   _____

Son's Signature   Date

Pray Together

Father, we ask You to do Your work in our relationship...in Your way and in Your timing. We need Your help and guidance as we take this step of faith to trust You to begin to pull back the hard layers of our hearts that have prevented us from hearing Your whisper. Teach us. Show us. Reveal to us the areas that need the healing touch of Jesus. We are expecting great things because we serve a great God. Have Your way with us, Lord Jesus Christ. Come, Holy Spirit. Amen.

1

EVERYBODY'S DOING IT

Go against the flow.

If you decide to just go with the flow, you'll end up where the flow goes, which is usually downhill, often leading to a big pile of sludge and a life of unhappiness. You'll end up doing what everyone else is doing.

–Sean Covey

As a kid, I remember trying to convince my mom and dad that I should be allowed to do something because all my friends were doing it. Their parents were permitting it (either they were lying or their parents never knew about it), but my parents would end the conversation with, "If all your friends were jumping off a bridge, should we let you do that too?" It was tough to overcome that argument. They always said that we weren't going to be like everybody else and we would do things differently. They assured me that in the long run that would be a good thing. Now as a parent, I find myself saying the same things. It turns out they were right.

Every young man feels this tension of fitting into the crowd or going with the flow. Most boys feel pressure to be liked or fit in with the "cool" kids, and many will compromise their standards and stop doing "the right thing," particularly when it comes to using foul language, talking inappropriately about girls, laughing at foul jokes, and watching videos. It eventually moves into the areas of alcohol, drugs, and sex. This tension doesn't stop when you become a man. In some ways peer pressure gets stronger every year.

Fitting in takes no effort.

God calls us to do things differently. If we do life the way everybody else does, we will get the life that everybody else has. Following the crowd is easy. We instantly feel accepted and part of the group without struggle or tension. When we do what everybody else is doing, we are destined for mediocrity. The majority doesn't strive for excellence, because they drop their standards and ambitions to the lowest common denominator. Going with the flow never produces greatness. In the crowd are missed opportunities, unrealized potential, and regrets.

Jesus expects more of us.

Jesus wants us to stand up and stand out. He wants us to go against the flow. He wants us to be the one who stands instead of bowing down to the idols of the day. He wants us to be the one who isn't afraid to pray in the restaurant when no one else is praying before they eat. He wants us to rise early and start our day in the Word, seeking Him, while our friends soak up one more hour of sleep. He wants us to live with a sense of mission and passion and go against the flow of our culture. All the great leaders of God swam upstream.

Take your everyday, ordinary life—your sleeping, eating, going-to-work, and walking-around life—and place it before

God as an offering. Embracing what God does for you is the best thing you can do for him. Don't become so well adjusted to your culture that you fit into it without even thinking. Instead, fix your attention on God. You'll be changed from the inside out. –Romans 12:1–2 MSG

God calls us to go against the flow. So look around. What is everybody else doing? Are they taking care of their health, or are they eating junk? Are they entertained by garbage on TV or at the movies, or are they protecting their heart by shielding their eyes? Are they engaging in gossip and inappropriate jokes at the expense of others? Chances are good that if everybody is doing it, you probably shouldn't. If your life looks like everybody else's, ask yourself two questions: *Why?* and *Is that a good thing, or does something need to change?*

There are three great blessings when we go against the flow:

1. **God will be glorified.**
   When we go against the flow, we position ourselves for God to work in the most unlikely ways. When we go against the flow, God's power is displayed in us so His fame can be spread through us. God gets the credit, not us.

2. **Greatness is produced.**
   Going with the flow produces mediocracy, never greatness. Going against the flow will always produce strength, courage, tenacity, and boldness. It feels good to be different, especially when you know you're doing it God's way.

3. **God is pleased.**
   God delights when His children swim upstream with a little wiggle. Your earthly father does too. Any old dead fish can go with the flow, but only a living fish can go

against it. God is pleased when we are set apart for His service.

The cool thing is that being different can actually build your strength of character. Being different and choosing the higher road makes you stronger. Men of God have had to be different; they've had to take some heat for not giving in to pressure. They've all felt lonely and like outsiders in the group. Some days that really stinks. But they've learned that God's ways are always best.

One of the best things a father can do for his son is to model what it looks like to be different. Don't do what everybody else does. Find key decisions to make that are different—like not drinking, or choosing to spend time with the family instead of out with "the guys." And then invest that time with your son, reinforcing his strength to be different and rewarding who he is becoming as a young man. Celebrate that you are in it together.

We are called to greatness.

We live by a different standard. We must be willing to take the narrow road that leads to life without compromise. Don't do what everybody else is doing. Come together as father and son and decide to do things differently together. The godly life requires that we go against the flow.

TAKE ACTION

1. Are you going with the flow or against the flow? In what ways does your life look like everybody else's? In what ways is it different?

2. Why is it hard to swim upstream? What role does peer pressure play?

3. What are some key areas where you need to change direction and go against the flow? List them and share with each other. Decide what you can do differently together and form a pact to stick together.

Father, help us to find ways to go against the flow. Give us the courage we will need to do the right thing and be different, especially when it requires that we stand alone. Build a bond between us that celebrates that we are different and doing life Your way. Amen.

2

EYE-POPPING GRACE

CALLED TO GREATNESS PRINCIPLE
Grace is getting the good we don't deserve.

I do not understand the mystery of grace—only that it meets us where we are and does not leave us where it found us.

–Anne Lamott

Floyd Harris gave me the same reply every time I asked him how he was doing. It was his trademark saying: "Better than I deserve." The first time he said it to me, I was confused, so I asked him what he meant. He had a one-word answer: "Grace." Floyd was a godly eighty-year-old man who knew that the secret to life was to live by grace. I have often used the "Floydian" reply myself, and I typically receive the same response that I gave to Floyd.

And God is able to make every grace overflow to you, so that in every way, always having everything you need, you may excel in every good work. –2 Corinthians 9:8 HCSB

Being in the church my entire life, I have been around the word *grace* a lot. I memorized verses, sang hymns, heard sermons, and read books. I bumped into grace often but rarely took time to understand it. Yes, I know that grace is God's lavish favor on undeserving sinners, but grace also redeems me, reforms me, and rewards me—even though I don't deserve it. God revealed to me that grace is not only amazing when we receive it but also eye-popping when we give it.

> Grace first needs to be received.

Grace can only be experienced if we receive it. It is clear in Ephesians 2:8–9 that it is by grace that we are saved through faith: "God saved you by his grace when you believed. And you can't take credit for this; it is a gift from God. Salvation is not a reward for the good things we have done, so none of us can boast about it."

We don't deserve to be saved, but it is through God's grace upon us that we can receive salvation. As a teenager, I experienced God's grace when I surrendered my life to Him. I did absolutely nothing to deserve salvation. Zip. Zero. Nada. However, experiencing the fullness of grace is not a one-time experience at salvation. God's grace is available to receive every day. It's hard to swallow the fact that He actually rewards us for our puny efforts to serve and please Him.

It is interesting that most Christians use *mercy* and *grace* interchangeably. There is a huge difference. *Mercy* is not getting the bad that we deserve, which I am abundantly grateful for. However, *grace* is getting the good we don't deserve. I think it is easier for us to embrace and understand mercy over grace, but God wants us to fully experience His grace daily because He is good, gracious, and generous.

Grace is hard for us to receive because we know we don't deserve it. The sin in our lives often prevents us from completely embracing the fullness of grace. Brennan Manning nailed it when he wrote, "To live by grace means to acknowledge my whole life story, the light side and the dark. In admitting my shadow side I learn who I am and what God's grace means."

Grace needs to be given.

Once we receive and experience grace, we must give it to others. This gets messy, because we usually want to give grace to those who deserve it, not to those who don't. However, when I extend God's grace to others, it becomes an eye-popping, surprising grace. I have learned that giving God's grace transforms me in two ways:

1. **Grace shatters a judgmental spirit.**
   The Lord revealed to me that I put people into two boxes. The Just-Like-Me box holds the people I like and gravitate toward. I will give them lots of grace. The Not-Like-Me box holds people whom I don't understand and thus stay away from. I don't offer them grace, which is judgmental. I'm embarrassed how I judge people. All throughout last year, the Lord painfully taught me to extend grace to all—in the same way He does. No picking and choosing who gets it. No boxes. Just extending the same grace I have received from Him. When I do that, grace becomes eye-popping.

2. **Grace unleashes a generous spirit.**
   Max Lucado, in his book *Grace*, says, "Let grace unscrooge your heart. Grace walks in the front door and selfishness scampers out the back. It changes the heart." When we extend amazing grace, it unleashes amazing generosity. We get to lavish favor on the undeserving by

being the hands and feet of Jesus. This is when grace gets fun.

Growing in grace is a daily process. In 2 Peter 3:18 HCSB, we are reminded of this truth: "But grow in the grace and knowledge of our Lord and Savior Jesus Christ. To Him be the glory both now and to the day of eternity. Amen."

As fathers and sons, our goal should be to receive and give eye-popping grace. It's easy for me to teach my son about hard work, commitment, and perseverance. When it comes to grace, it's hard. The best way is for me to model a life of grace—receiving and giving grace. Knowing that God's grace is bottomless, I also need to extend bottomless grace to him. No strings attached. No motives. Just eye-popping grace.

Grace changes us and others. Receiving grace is getting what we don't deserve, and giving grace is giving to others what they don't deserve. Lord, thank You for the gift of grace.

TAKE ACTION

1. Why is it important to know the difference between mercy and grace? Which one is easier for you to embrace?

2. How has grace impacted your life?

3. When do you experience God's amazing grace the most?

4. How have you extended God's grace? Is your heart unscrooged?

5. What are practical ways that you help each other understand the fullness of God's grace?

Father, thank You for Your grace that You generously pour out. Help me to receive the fullness of grace every day. Thank You for Your lavish favor on me, an undeserving sinner. Your grace redeems me, reforms me, and rewards me. Let Your grace shatter my judgmental spirit. Also, show me how to give grace to others. In Jesus' name, amen.

3

FIRE IN THE BELLY

The fire within comes from Him.

The words are fire in my belly, a burning in my bones.
I'm worn out trying to hold it in. I can't do it any longer!
—Jeremiah 20:9 MSG

"Do you have fire in your belly?" is a question I've heard hundreds of times from coaches. It was never a question that I was supposed to answer, but rather a challenge to play with passion. Basically, coaches wanted to know if I had what it takes. They always wanted to know if I had the determination and commitment to play with the competitive edge. As an athlete, I never had the natural ability of others (speed, strength, size), but I did have the fire in my belly that helped me excel athletically.

My dad taught me about living and playing with passion at a very young age—the ability to dig in and make every moment count. The work ethic he taught me carried over into every aspect of my life. He was intentional about showing me what it took to have tenacity—the unwavering discipline to persevere. He modeled it for me in his own life. He had drive and discipline that my brothers and I caught and still live with today.

For me, the fire was hustle and grit to get the job done—whatever the coach asked of me. I was the player who always played at 100 percent until the whistle blew. My goal was to leave it all on the field during practices and games. No cutting corners and no plays off. It also carried over into my training time when no one was watching. The fire burned strong and helped me put in hundreds of hours running sprints, lifting weights, and doing push-ups and sit-ups.

I'm thankful for the example my dad gave me. The fire wasn't just taught but also caught. It was the very thing that helped me play lacrosse at the college and professional level. I'm thankful that I now coach my son's high school lacrosse team and show him what fire in the belly is all about. And he gets it.

It's one thing to talk about fire in the belly when it comes to sports, but it's another thing to talk about fire in the belly when it comes to our spiritual life. In Jeremiah 20:9, Jeremiah says that he had a fire burning so strong for God that he couldn't contain it. He was worn out trying to hold it in. The spiritual hustle, the spiritual grit, and the spiritual tenacity all need to burn within us so strong that we can't hold them back.

Imagine finally confessing to someone, "I just can't keep it from you any longer. It has to come out. I'm tired of withholding Jesus from you. It's burning so strongly inside of me that I have no option but to share Jesus with you." That would be incredible.

Peter and John are great examples of this. In Acts 3, Peter encountered a man who was lame from birth and had to be carried in to the temple. Peter healed this man in the name of Jesus, and the man's feet and ankles were instantly healed and strengthened. Peter was "fired up" and began to preach boldly, addressing those who had just witnessed this miracle and many more,

> Now repent of your sins and turn to God, so that your sins may be wiped away. Then times of refreshment will come from the presence of the Lord, and he will again send you Jesus, your appointed Messiah. —Acts 3:19–20

Many who heard the message believed it. Peter and John were taken to jail and faced the religious council the next day. They answered the council's demands by saying,

> We cannot stop telling about everything we have seen and heard. —Acts 4:20

That is fire in the belly. The fire was the presence of the Holy Spirit. Our passion for our Lord should be like a fire that rages within. However, we must also remember that the fire within comes from Him. We must lay ourselves on the altar and ask God to consume us with His fire. The great preacher John Wesley said that large crowds came to hear him preach during the Great Awakening because "I set myself on fire, and the people come to see me burn."

One of the greatest things we can teach our sons is to have an authentic passion for Jesus. Passion for Jesus is stoked like you stoke a fire, by consistently adding wood. We add wood spiritually by serving others and taking risks to share our faith and love people. Putting our faith into action in our everyday walk keeps it burning. Spending personal time with the Lord adds wood and stokes the fire too. It needs to be demonstrated more than taught. In a good way, I feel the weight of responsibility to spend time every day with the Lord, as an example for my son. If he sees me cultivating the fire in my spiritual disciplines at home but the fire is never burning when I'm with other people, then I would be a fake. My prayer is that my son would see me getting close to Jesus and living it in a powerful way every day.

Are you on fire for Jesus? Do others want to come and see you burn for Jesus?

TAKE ACTION

1. What do you think of when you hear the phrase "spiritual fire in the belly"? Why?

2. What does it mean to have spiritual grit and tenacity?

3. How do you burn for Jesus every day? Share ways that you can add wood to the fire through private disciplines and public exercises of faith.

4. Read Psalm 84:1–2. Pray this passage as a prayer for each other.

Lord, I desire for Your fire to burn within me. I want to have a spiritual fire in the belly that can't be contained. Consume me with Your fire. Let the fire that burns within be a light in the darkness that surrounds me. Amen.

T AKE
M Y W HEEL

Stay close to Jesus.

Come close to God, and God will come close to you.

–James 4:8

or years now, a bunch of dads in the neighborhood get together and go cycling. Many times I would take my older boys along for the ride. When riding in a group, there are some very important guidelines to follow to ensure that no one makes an unexpected movement that causes a crash. Most of us have learned these lessons the hard way. Believe me when I tell you that nobody wants to fall and get road rash. Hand signals for turns and to warn of obstacles are huge, and verbal commands give critical information regarding other vehicles.

But one of the most important aspects of riding together is the distance kept between the rear wheel of the rider ahead of you and the front wheel of your bike. Keeping the right distance prevents accidents, but more importantly keeps the riders together as they pick up speed.

"Take my wheel" is a common instruction from the strongest

rider in the group. The first rider has to work harder than the rest because he or she encounters most of the wind resistance; this is called drafting. The riders who follow have less resistance, and it's easier to keep the pace if they stay close enough. The optimal distance is less than twenty-four inches apart—rear wheel to front wheel of the next rider—depending on the speed of the group. If you fall behind more than six to eight feet, you may have to work like crazy to hang on as the line picks up speed.

The closer you stay to the optimal distance, the better the ride. This same principle holds true in our lives. Fathers and sons need to stay close to one another as they both stay close to God. At the start of every day, I can almost hear Jesus say, "Take My wheel." In my life, the closer I stay to Jesus, the easier it is to hear and see the instruction I need for daily decisions.

The Bible gives us countless examples of people who took God's wheel and stayed close to Him. In Genesis, we read the stories of two godly men, Enoch and Noah.

> Enoch lived 365 years, walking in close fellowship with God.
> –Genesis 5:23–24

> Noah was a righteous man, the only blameless person living on earth at the time, and he walked in close fellowship with God. –Genesis 6:9

Both of these men stayed in close fellowship with God, and He used them in mighty ways for generations to come. He even saved humanity through Noah, his wife, and his three sons and daughters-in-law when he rescued them from the flood.

Intimacy in our relationship with God doesn't happen if we grow apart. The farther away we get, the harder it is to hear His voice, follow His path, and keep His pace. We need to stay as close as possible or we'll have to work like crazy to hang on.

Peter discovered the problem of distance personally when Jesus was arrested:

> But Peter followed him at a distance, right up to the court-yard of the high priest. He entered and sat down with the guards to see the outcome. —Matthew 26:58 NIV

Peter was afraid he might be arrested too, so he kept his distance. Earlier, Peter had told Jesus, "Even if all fall away on account of you, I never will.... Even if I have to die with you, I will never disown you" (Matthew 26:33, 35 NIV). Then he stood side-by-side with Him, defending Jesus after Judas betrayed Him, cutting off the ear of one of the servants of the high priest. Peter was bold when he was close to Jesus, but full of fear when he followed at a distance. He denied Jesus three times from a distance. I doubt that Peter would have done so if he had remained close to Him, but we'll never know.

Distance divides relationships.

The story of the prodigal son is another example of what happens when distance brings division. The younger of two sons asked his father for his inheritance now instead of waiting until his father died. The dad gave him his portion of the wealth.

> Not long after that, the younger son got together all he had, set off for a distant country and there squandered his wealth in wild living. —Luke 15:13 NIV

The son was distant from his father even before he left—he cared more about receiving an inheritance of money than receiving a legacy of love. The distance of his heart caused him to leave and lose it all. But all the while, the father waited expectantly for his son to come back. When he did, love was restored.

Dads, we need to take the lead and take God's wheel. We need to show our sons what it looks like to take His wheel every day in every situation we face. Starting the day with devotions, time in God's Word, and prayer and praise sets the example. Paying attention to His signals and signs throughout the day does too. Sons, you need to take your father's wheel and do what he does. Keep the pace. Don't lose his wheel or you might lose your way. If we let distance grow between us because of discipline, conflict, or criticism, or if we allow the distractions of too much work or the isolation of technology, it will end badly.

> Stay close to God; stay close to each other.

That's the bottom line. Start the day seeking God together. Take His wheel right from the start. Don't just model it, do it together. Don't let anything come between you. When we come close to God, He comes close to us.

TAKE ACTION

1. On a scale of 1 to 10, rate how close you are to God right now. Share why.

2. On that same scale, rate how close you are to each other. Why do you feel that way?

3. Read Psalm 23:4 and Psalm 34:18. What do these verses tell us about God when times are toughest?

4. Read Psalm 148:18. What do we have to do to get close to God?

5. Dads and sons, what is one thing that each of you can do to create closeness in your relationship with God and each other?

Father, keep me and my dad/son close. Help us to take Your wheel together and follow close behind. Remove any distractions or obstacles that are preventing us from staying close to You and each other. Help us be intentional and determined to stay close to Jesus. Amen.

5

Warrior Mind-Set

CALLED TO GREATNESS PRINCIPLE
Be strong and courageous.

*I learned that courage was not the absence of fear, but
the triumph over it. The brave man is not he who does
not feel afraid, but he who conquers that fear.*

–Nelson Mandela

When the boys were little, they would dress up in their military camouflage and I would take them through a mini boot camp, making them salute and "give me ten!" push-ups. They loved it. They would play army all around the house and yard and had the tiny soldiers everywhere. We even painted their room camo, put up military nets, and hung B-2 bombers from the ceiling. Over the years their warrior mind-set showed up on the athletic fields, in the classroom, and as they faced obstacles and challenges in a variety of ways. If the military needed a few good men, I was getting them ready.

The United States Special Operations Forces (SOF) have this warrior mind-set and they inspire me. They are the most highly trained, disciplined, capable, and mission-driven people in the world. They serve in many capacities all around the world to fight for and defend freedom. The SOF we're probably most familiar with is the Navy SEALs, but every branch of the military has one. They enter the most dangerous circumstances and complete the most extreme missions. Knowing they are there helps me sleep better at night.

These warriors complete the most difficult training in the world so they are fully prepared for the battlefield—mentally, physically, emotionally, and spiritually. They have an internal quest for greatness; they desire to push their body, mind, and soul to its very limits. They are fully prepared because they know what's at stake.

These soldiers have the warrior mind-set and are strong and courageous. I love the focus, determination, and discipline, but I'm super challenged by their mental toughness and their internal voice that says, *I will never back down, give in, or give up! Excuses are unacceptable. Failure is not an option.* They always focus on the three things they can control—their attitude, effort, and emotions. Mental toughness surfaces in how you respond when the going gets tough. When things are going the worst, will you bring your best? Will you choose to respond with a positive attitude, composure, and energy?

When I consider what they have to do just to make the cut, the adversity they've overcome, and the obstacles they've cleared, they stretch what I believe is possible. It's almost like a fire is ignited in my spirit to pursue excellence and to find that edge of what I am capable of doing.

I believe that in our culture, men need to return to the warrior mind-set with supernatural strength and courage from God's promise that He will be with us wherever we go. Courage isn't the absence of fear; it's taking action in the face of fear.

Life will bring adversity, and we need to be fully prepared and ready.

> This is my command—be strong and courageous! Do not be afraid or discouraged. For the LORD your God is with you wherever you go. –Joshua 1:9

After the death of Moses, Joshua was chosen by God to lead His people into the Promised Land. He had spent forty years preparing Joshua for this moment. But the task must have seemed impossible. God knew Joshua would face fear and doubt and a sense of inadequacy; that's why He gave him courage and the warrior mind-set by promising His presence. God knew Joshua would face incredible opposition. He knew there would be challenges that seemed insurmountable. He also knew he would feel pressure from his own people along the way.

> I have told you these things, so that in me you may have peace. In this world you will have trouble. But take heart! I have overcome the world. –John 16:33 NIV

Fathers and sons are under a lot of pressure these days. It's difficult to have courage in life when facing difficult challenges and circumstances. When times are toughest, we need to rely on God the most. We can live with strength and courage because Jesus has overcome the world. There is no challenge we will ever face that He cannot overcome. Knowing this brings confidence and peace to everyone who trusts in Him.

> The LORD is a warrior; the LORD is his name!
> –Exodus 15:3 NIV

We must be prepared. That's why God encourages us to take on the warrior mind-set. Our thoughts determine how we feel and that drives what we do. It all starts in the mind.

So here's the warrior mind-set:

1. **I refuse to make excuses.**
   Take out the trash and take in the truth. Remove negative thinking and replace it with what's possible. Take responsibility for what you can do, and stop complaining about what you can't. Read 2 Corinthians 10:5.

2. **I revel in the toughest circumstances.**
   Anticipate challenges and obstacles. Be willing to enter the "crucible" so you can be refined, tested, and proven. In adversity, warriors say, "I'm made for this." Read John 16:33.

3. **I recover from setbacks.**
   When something goes wrong, a warrior says, "What can I do to fix it?" Put disappointments behind you quickly and move forward. Keep your eyes on Jesus. Forget the past and stay focused on the finish line. Train your brain to reject doubt, discouragement, and defeat. Read Philippians 3:13–14.

4. **I rely on His presence and power.**
   In our own strength we are limited. But when we trust God for direction, wisdom, and strength, nothing is impossible. Read Luke 1:37.

Can you imagine if all dads and sons developed a mental toughness and were able to step up and step out with boldness and courage? What if we looked at challenges as confirmation that we are right where God wants us for a reason? What if instead of running away at the first sign of trouble or when we encounter obstacles, we saw them as opportunities to be great? Fathers, encourage your sons to rise again from difficulties.

It's time to take every thought captive and remind ourselves daily that God is with us—that nothing is impossible with God. We must be intentional in training our minds to overcome adversity, challenges, and setbacks. It's time to be strong and courageous.

TAKE ACTION

1. When facing challenges, do you typically make excuses or find a way?

2. What are some circumstances that test your attitude, emotions, and effort?

3. Do you have the warrior's mind-set? Share with each other why or why not.

Father, help us to refuse to make excuses, to revel in tough circumstances, recover from setbacks, and rely on Your presence and power. Give us the strength to be courageous in the face of adversity. Help us to remove negative thinking and problems and replace them with Your promises. Amen.

6

RUAVRP

CALLED TO GREATNESS PRINCIPLE
When you refresh, you bless.

Those who refresh others will themselves be refreshed.
–Proverbs 11:25

*I*n the last several years, there has been a worldwide outbreak of what could be the most deadly disease known to man. Experts say that it has the potential to wreak havoc on 100 percent of the world's population. Everyone is vulnerable because we're all exposed to those who carry it. This disease is called VDP Disease. Are you familiar with it? The World Health Organization has issued warnings detailing its devastating effects.

VDP Disease stands for "Very Draining Person" Disease, and it is carried and transmitted by VDPs around the world. You can identify VDPs by how they exhibit repetitive negative, pessimistic, complaining, and life-sucking behaviors. They are highly contagious; once you've been exposed to these people, you may not even realize that you now have the disease because you don't see the symptoms. You can't see VDP Disease in the mirror, but others can spot it from a mile away.

You've probably heard the expression "misery loves company." VDPs love to pull you down to their level of misery. It actually makes them feel better about themselves. They will take chunks of flesh out of you every time you encounter them. They criticize, complain, whine, make excuses, and find faults. Their words are laced with destruction, and they spew their poison on anyone who dares to listen. Those infected can be found everywhere—in neighborhoods, schools, sports fields, businesses, churches, and families. If you spot a VDP, run; if you don't, he or she will drain you of the positive energy you need for life.

The good news is this: there is one known cure for the VDP Disease. It's called VRP or "Very Refreshing People." Large numbers of faith-filled, positive, right-living, energized VRPs are needed to combat the devastating effects of Very Draining People. VRPs are more difficult to find, but every once in a while you can spot one because they bring healing and relief. When VRPs are around, you feel like a million bucks. They speak words of life into the ordinary and transform it. They re-fill your energy tank—emotionally, relationally, and spiritually. They breathe encouragement, blessing, and hope into your soul and remind you that nothing is impossible with God.

I have several friends who are VRPs. Every time I talk with them, I feel like I have a red cape on my back and a big "S" on my chest. They make me feel like Superman because they speak words of life into me—words drenched in hope. They aren't just make-you-feel-good words, but we-believe-in-you words. What a difference. They see God's greatness in me. They inspire me. Their encouragement isn't fake or artificial; it is powerful, purpose-filled edification.

> When you are refreshing, you are a blessing.

In the Bible, Onesiphorus was a VRP. He brought hope and healing. He's only mentioned twice, both times in 2 Timothy. Obviously, he's not a popular Bible character, but he was well-known to the apostle Paul because of the encouragement he delivered. In fact, his name actually means "to bring help or profit-bearing."

> May the Lord show mercy to the household of Onesiphorus, because he often refreshed me and was not ashamed of my chains. On the contrary, when he was in Rome, he searched hard for me until he found me. —2 Timothy 1:16–17 NIV

Everybody needs a VRP, and Onesiphorus was one of Paul's main VRPs. Paul was beaten down by VDPs, and some were his closest friends. He received the 360-degree pounding (from all sides) because when he made a stand for the Truth, an attack would always come.

From Onesiphorus' example, we learn three key characteristics of a VRP that we can apply as fathers and sons:

1. **Refreshment is repeated.**
   Paul writes, "he often refreshed me." This was not a one-and-done refreshing; Onesiphorus poured out encouragement time and time again. The word refreshed means "to brace up or revive by fresh air." When Onesiphorus arrived at the jail, Paul probably pumped his hands into the air and rejoiced, saying, "Yes! Thank God. He is here again." Refreshing needs to be regular and repeated.

2. **Refreshment is risky.**

Paul says that Onesiphorus "was not ashamed of my chains." He was willing to associate himself with Paul's sufferings in prison. During one of Paul's darkest hours in a Roman prison, Onesiphorus showed up. As a former slave, Onesiphorus risked his life by going into prison to refresh his brother in Christ. We need to step out of our comfort zone to refresh others. Refreshing others is often risky. Onesiphorus brought encouragement, hope, and life.

3. **Refreshment is relentless.**

Onesiphorus "searched hard" for Paul. He was relentless in finding his friend, and he did not stop until he "found him." Onesiphorus did whatever it took to bring a big dose of refreshment to Paul. VRPs are persistent and tenacious.

The question is—RUAVRP? Are you a Very Refreshing Person? The challenge is not whether you have VRPs in your life, but are you one? When you walk into the room, do people run or do they pump their fists into the air? Do you bring life to people? To your son? To your father?

Fathers need to set the standard for their sons. Your words can unlock God's greatness in your son. You need to be committed to infusing life into him through your intentional words of nourishment. Let him feast off your encouragement. Become a VRP for each other, because when you are refreshing, you are a blessing.

TAKE ACTION

1. Who do you know who is a Very Refreshing Person?
   How about a Very Draining Person?

2. If you asked your friends or family members, what
   would they say? Why?

3. On a scale of 1 to 10 (10 being a refresher and
   1 being a drainer), rank yourself. Rank each other.

4. Read Proverbs 12:18 and 18:21 together. What are
   some specific ways that you can develop into a VRP?

5. Do you see areas to refresh your son/father? Write
   those down and begin to breathe refreshment and
   blessing into each other's life.

*Father, there is fresh power at the foot of the cross.
I want to be refreshed by You and used to pour out
Your goodness to others. I want to be a lifter—a
refresher. Help me to be a Very Refreshing Person
every day. Too often I get focused on myself and do
not see the opportunities to bless others with words
and actions. Show me how I need to minister to
those with whom I interact. Thank You for loving me
and refreshing me all the time.*

7

ARE YOU KIDDING ME?

CALLED TO GREATNESS PRINCIPLE
Humility beats pride.

So I say, live by the Spirit, and you will not gratify the desires of the sinful nature. For the sinful nature desires what is contrary to the Spirit, and the Spirit what is contrary to the sinful nature. They are in conflict with each other, so that you do not do what you want.

–Galatians 5:16–17 NIV

Recently I was catching up on some NFL highlights when I saw an incredible play that made me scream, "Are you kidding me?" at the TV. But even though it was an extraordinary catch, it wasn't the great play that actually caused my reaction. It was what the player did after the play. With all eyes on him, he reached above his head and with both hands pointed to his name on the back of the jersey. I forgot his name (even though he wanted us all to remember it), but I didn't forget his gesture. Pride was oozing from him.

I yelled, "Are you kidding me?" in disgust more than once. I would have understood if he'd pointed to the team name on the front of his jersey. Or what if he pointed to the quarterback who'd threaded the needle with a perfect pass? What about the six offensive linemen who gave the quarterback time to find the open receiver? Or the coaches who called the perfect play? But he made it all about him. The truth is, that gesture is common, accepted, and goes virtually unnoticed today.

On the other hand, I enjoyed what Matt Stover, former NFL kicker, would do after every kick. He always pointed to the sky regardless of whether he made it or missed. It was his way to glorify God and also remain humble. Matt, like many athletes today, recognized that God gave him the ability to play and pointed to the sky as a regular reminder.

We have grown so numb to self-centered people that we don't even notice the behavior in ourselves. When people acknowledge the impact we're making for Christ, we point to our name on the back of the jersey. God was actually speaking to me when that receiver pointed to his name on the back of his jersey. I felt the Lord was saying to me, "Dan, you don't outwardly point to your name on your jersey, but you do it inwardly. You want people to notice you. You think you are better than this receiver because you don't externally point to your name, but take a look inside." The Lord convicted me through this athlete's selfish behavior. I heard the Lord saying to me the same thing I'd said to the player: "Are you kidding Me?"

I was a hypocrite and I knew it. Outwardly I looked humble, but inwardly I was full of pride. I felt important and better than others. Humility is not thinking less of yourself, but thinking of yourself less. It's putting others first. And I was convicted by God's Word:

> Don't be selfish; don't try to impress others. Be humble, thinking of others as better than yourselves. –Philippians 2:3

As men of God, we must put on humility every day just like we put on our clothes. We must never consider leaving home without clothing ourselves with humility. It is an act of our will, a decision that we need to make daily to put our heart in the right place.

> Since God chose you to be the holy people he loves, you must clothe yourselves with tenderhearted mercy, kindness, humility, gentleness, and patience. —Colossians 3:12

It's our goal to get to the place of entire dependence upon God. We need to put down our rights and pick up our responsibilities instead. If Jesus could give up His place in heaven to come to those He created, then we can give up our pride. If He was willing to sacrifice and suffer for our benefit, can't we sacrifice the spotlight and enjoy lifting others up? It will produce an inward satisfaction that is hard to describe. We've always said that we shouldn't be the one who tells everybody how great we are and that if there's any positive talk, we should let it come from somebody else.

As fathers and sons, we need to understand that pursuing humility is a lifetime thing. Here's a simple list to review together that shows the value of humility over pride:

HUMILITY	PRIDE
Virtue	Vice
Reveals	Blinds
Secure	Insecure
Attractive	Obnoxious
Confident	Arrogant
Responsive	Resistant
Selfless	Selfish
Fruit of the Spirit	Sin

The blessing of humility is intimacy. When we clothe ourselves with humility, there is greater intimacy with Jesus and with others. Pride divides. Humility unites. Pride pushes God and others away. Humility unifies relationships. Fathers, don't let pride drive a wedge between you and your son. Put your son before yourself. Put on humility and watch how God will bless your relationship.

Fathers and sons, die to self. Never point to yourself, not even in the hidden areas of your heart. There needs to be a total sacrifice of the flesh, pointing toward God on the outside and on the inside. Your lives should bring attention to the only Famous One: Jesus Christ. Humility beats pride every single time.

TAKE ACTION

1. How does it make you feel when you see your name either on a jersey or in print? Be honest.

2. Why is our society consumed with the spotlight? Why is pride and selfishness so prevalent?

3. Name someone who is a great example of being humble and bringing attention to the Famous One.

4. Ask God to reveal the things in your life that are preventing you from giving Him all the glory.

5. Share with each other some practical ways you can point to God externally and internally.

Famous One, Lord Jesus, I want to make You great. I want to give You glory inwardly and outwardly. It is easy to give glory outwardly, but in the depths of my soul, there is a pride and selfishness that rises up and prevents me from laying it all at Your feet. I keep glory for myself. Help me, Lord, to give You all the glory all the time. Today, I die to myself so that You will live in and through me. In Jesus' name I pray, amen.

8

SUCCESSFUL FAILURE

CALLED TO GREATNESS PRINCIPLE
God turns failure into success.

Failure is not an option.
—Gene Kranz, Apollo 13 flight director (NASA)

"Houston, we have a problem." These famous words were said by Jim Lovell, the mission commander for NASA's Apollo 13, back in April 1970 as the space flight crew was on its way to the moon. In the days before launch, as he prepared for the mission, Jim said he'd never felt more confident; after all, he had logged over 572 hours in space already and this would be the USA's third time landing on the moon if all went well. But on April 13, just nine minutes after signing off for the night and two hundred thousand miles from earth, disaster struck. An oxygen tank exploded, causing substantial damage and sparking a series of events that put the crew in grave danger.

> Sometimes the mission we start with
> isn't the one we finish with.

From that moment on, the mission to land on the moon was over; the new mission was survival. Would the three-man crew be able to return safely to earth? If the flight crew were to have a shot, the ground crew at Mission Control in Houston would need a miracle. Gene Kranz, Apollo 13 flight director in Houston, would not accept failure.

On day three they knew the mission would be a failure. When they returned safely to earth, it was renamed NASA's "successful failure." They had survived extreme cold, sleep deprivation, dehydration, lack of oxygen, and food rationing, all while making repairs and modifications to the spacecraft as directed by Houston. These courageous men and women had turned failure into success.

> God loves to turn our failure into success.

God loves to turn defeat into victory, disappointment into determination, challenges into character. That's what our Heavenly Father does. In fact, the Bible is full of stories of successful failures. A successful failure is when you fail while attempting something big for God, but then look for God to turn that failure into future success. You choose to look at failure differently. You refuse to let it define you or discourage you. You don't wallow in it and beat yourself up. Instead, you see the failure as an opportunity to learn and grow. You know it's all a matter of perspective and choose to find:

- opportunities for every obstacle;
- possibilities for every problem; and
- stepping stones for every stumbling block.

Many years ago, one of my boys earned a spot on a top-level lacrosse team. The coach had a reputation of being hard on his players, but it was a big deal to make the team. Practices were an immediate challenge and the coach demoralized him. He made my son feel like he was out of his league and pulled him out every time he made a mistake. Instead of instructing him on what to do to get better, he beat him up verbally. After a while, this boy who loved lacrosse never wanted to play again. He was afraid to make mistakes and began to "dog it" in the drills.

I encouraged him to look at the situation differently—to use the adversity to get better, to be the best teammate, to do all the little things, to go all-out, and to have the best attitude on the team. He worked hard and had a positive attitude. The coach noticed, and even though my son still rarely saw the field, he used this "failure" to prove to himself what he was really made of. This experience helped make him into an all-conference player his senior year, but best of all it helped develop and refine his character.

> As we risk failure,
> God promises to use failure if it happens.

Those who experience successful failures have the courage to risk failure while daring greatly and then use failure to fuel success. And good dads always use failure to fuel future success. Take Peter, for example. He wanted to do great things but experienced failure along the way. He was willing to take big risks without being sure of success, and he didn't always get it right.

When the disciples saw Jesus walking on the water in the midst of a storm, Peter was the only one to dare greatly and step out of the boat.

But when he saw the strong wind and the waves, he was terrified and began to sink. "Save me, Lord!" he shouted. Jesus immediately reached out and grabbed him. "You have so little faith," Jesus said. "Why did you doubt me?" –Matthew 14:30–31

Peter dared greatly and risked failure; Jesus used that failure to expand Peter's faith in what was possible with God. He wasn't defeated; instead, he became even more determined to trust Jesus fully. He didn't focus on the failure, but on his future. It's the role of the father to focus on what worked and not what went wrong. Dwelling on the small failure instead of the big success is a missed opportunity to create a close relationship. Building on the bright side is always best.

Later, when Jesus was betrayed by Judas, Peter defended Him with the sword. Peter was the only one who took action. He acted courageously, but he got it wrong. Jesus corrected his action immediately. It's the role of the father to help the son see the future in the midst of a failure. We have to be there to help him see the good that can come of it when he gets it wrong.

As fathers and sons, things don't always turn out like we want. Things don't always go as planned. Sometimes we shoot for the moon and land back on earth. One mission may fail—or the mission may unexpectedly change in the middle. How we react and respond to change and adversity determines how the story ends. God has purpose in every detour, disappointment, and failure. But with God, ultimate failure is not an option. God is ready to turn what we might consider our worst failure into our greatest victory. Don't let failure define or defeat you. Instead, let God turn your circumstances into successful failures.

TAKE ACTION

1. Have you ever tried something big or new and failed? Describe that experience.

2. Read Romans 8:28 and Philippians 1:6. What do these passages tell you about what God will do with us, even our failures?

3. What are some things that would make you risk failure while "daring greatly" for God? List them here.

4. Today, take a risk together and see what God does.

Father, thank You for seeing our bright future in the midst of our failures. Help us to dare greatly and take risks to do good things. Help us to see where we fall short as an opportunity to come together as father and son; let us be willing to risk failure, knowing that You will do great things as we go for it, even if things don't go quite as planned. Amen.

9

All-In

CALLED TO GREATNESS PRINCIPLE
Hold nothing back.

You've got to know what's most important and then give it all you've got.

–Lee Iaccoca

We've started a tradition in our family that when my boys turn eighteen, I take them skydiving. And I've already made the leap with my oldest two. Each time, as we got to the jump site, we both had to read through several pages of disclaimers and warnings so we would understand all the risks associated with jumping out of a plane at eleven thousand feet with only a parachute to help us land safely. We must have signed in a dozen spots. The final warning is printed on a bright red sheet of paper with a bold *WARNING* across the top and a reminder that we could die doing this. Each one of us took a deep breath, signed our name, and prepared to board the tiny plane. We watched as the diving pros prepared the parachutes, listening carefully to their instructions.

As we hopped on the plane, we knew we were fully committed. Once we were in the air, there would be no turning back—we'd be "all-in." So when the plane reached the full altitude, the door swung open and one at a time we each stepped out on a two-foot-by-two-foot platform and fell forward out of the plane. I was the second to go each time, so it was absolutely crazy to watch my son disappear into the sky below, heading toward the earth at 120 mph. As I jumped, it was amazing—both terrifying and exhilarating all at the same time.

> Hold nothing back;
> risk everything.

Talk about belief. Talk about confidence. Talk about courage and commitment. Some would call us crazy (and they'd probably be right). We believed that the skydiving experts knew what they were doing as they prepared the chutes and gave us instructions. We trusted the fact that each of them had over one thousand jumps each. We believed that we'd ultimately make it back to the ground safely and in one piece. Being all-in requires belief, faith, and action. If you don't put what you believe or trust into action, it's really meaningless.

Being all-in will often require taking a risk as well. It will push you out of your comfort zone and away from your ability to control every circumstance. Many things in life will be beyond your control, so it's a good idea to get used to it and start developing your faith.

> Behavior always follows belief.

We will do almost anything for what we deeply believe in. We will make sacrifices, work harder, and do whatever it takes for something we truly believe in. In Colossians 3:17 NIV, Paul talks about being all-in:

And whatever you do, whether in word or deed, do it all in the name of the Lord Jesus, giving thanks to God the Father through him.

Paul is saying that everything we say and do—when we eat, when we sleep, when we work, when we speak, when we serve others, even when we're just walking around—should demonstrate our belief in and love for Jesus. This includes our attitudes and actions; we hold absolutely nothing back.

In our culture, it can be challenging to be all-in for Jesus. For some reason, men and boys who are sold-out for their faith are seen as soft. But being all-in for Jesus takes incredible strength. It doesn't mean we lose our competitive edge; it's quite the opposite. We now want to win in ways that really matter.

When Jesus touches you, He moves you from all-out to all-in. That's exactly what happened to a man named Zacchaeus when he put his faith in Jesus. Zacchaeus was very short, very rich, and known as a "notorious sinner." He was a chief tax collector who made his money by charging as much as he could above and beyond what was required by the Romans. He was essentially a cheat, getting rich off his own people.

Are you all-out or all-in?

The Jewish people considered him an outcast; they kept him all-out, but Jesus called him to be all-in. Zacchaeus had to climb a tree to get a look at Jesus. Jesus saw him, called him by name, and then invited Himself to be a guest at his home that night.

His relationship with Jesus compelled him to be all-in. Zacchaeus was obviously overwhelmed that he had been accepted by Jesus, and he placed his faith and life in Jesus' hands. He held nothing back, not even his great wealth.

Zacchaeus stood before the Lord and said, "I will give half my wealth to the poor, Lord, and if I have cheated people on their taxes, I will give them back four times as much!" Jesus responded, "Salvation has come to this home today, for this man has shown himself to be a true son of Abraham."
–Luke 19:8–9

Jesus is telling us to be all-in. Our homes and communities need us as fathers and sons to be all-in. When we deeply believe that Jesus gave His all to save us, we give our all to live for Him. Zacchaeus was willing to make a huge financial sacrifice to do the right thing and demonstrate his belief. When we deeply believe that God's ways are the best ways, we will not compromise. When we truly believe that Jesus is what others need, we will share our testimony boldly regardless of what people think. We don't shy away from our Savior; instead, we become bolder in bringing faith into the conversation and showing His love by serving. When we believe that "whatever I do" should glorify God, it changes our behavior.

So let's show our love for Jesus by being all-in and holding nothing back.

TAKE ACTION

1. What does it mean to be all-in for Jesus?

2. Read Galatians 2:20. How can this verse help you surrender everything to Jesus?

3. What areas of your life are you holding back and struggling to give Jesus control over? List them here. Share the list with each other. Together pick one thing that you can take action on.

Father, help us to be all-in. Grow boldness within us to share our growing faith and serve others. Help us use everything we have—our time, energy, money, and words—for the benefit of others and to build Your kingdom. Amen.

10

RUBBER BAND FAITH

CALLED TO GREATNESS PRINCIPLE
Real faith stretches us.

*When Jesus heard this, he was astonished and said
to those following him, "I tell you the truth, I have not
found anyone in Israel with such great faith."*
—Matthew 8:10 NIV

have always loved rubber bands. They're one of the greatest inventions ever! They're simple, practical, and useful. There are many names for this wonderful invention: elastic band, lackey band, and my favorite, gumband. Everybody knows what a rubber band is—a short length of rubber and latex formed in the shape of a loop. It can have many uses, but simply put, it stretches to hold objects together. It's hard for me to imagine life without rubber bands.

I always keep a rubber band around my wrist. But my simple habit took on new meaning when I noticed a friend of mine also wearing one. When I asked him why he wore a rubber band, he said, "It's a constant reminder that God wants to stretch me daily." He shared with me that rubber bands are pretty useless unless they're stretched; when they're extended beyond their standard form, they can hold things together and accomplish their purpose. After hearing my friend's reasoning, my rubber band took on a whole new meaning.

> Faith is not really faith until it's stretched;
> it needs to be tested.

And when it's tested, it heats up. When a rubber band is stretched, it also produces heat. Try pressing it against your lips while stretching it. You will feel heat, and then releasing it will cause it to cool (I bet you'll try it after you read this). When we step out of our comfort zone and need God to show up, our faith heats up, grows, and expands.

Jesus was astonished only twice in Scripture: once by great faith and once by lack of faith. In Matthew 8:5–10, we see rubber band faith. The Roman commander had so much faith in Jesus, he asked Him to forgo the journey and just say the words to heal his servant. Jesus said He had never seen such great faith. Full faith. Super faith. Big faith. Bet-the-farm faith. Powerful faith. Rubber band faith. In Mark 6:4–6, we see the exact opposite as Jesus was unable to perform many miracles in the synagogue because of the lack of faith there.

> Faith, like a rubber band,
> is useless unless it's stretched.

Now the solo rubber band on my wrist is a constant reminder to have rubber band faith.

Recently, my son also started to wear a rubber band around his wrist. It's a powerful reminder to both of us that we want to be men of God who want to be stretched by God. Many times we just look at each other and simply pull on our rubber bands and remember our desire to have rubber band faith.

Is your faith getting stronger as the years go by? Is it growing or declining? When you're willing to step out and stretch yourself, God shows up and does what you can't do. That is rubber band faith! We need to keep putting ourselves in situations where we whisper, "God, if You don't show up, I am bound to fail."

In 2002, I was presented with one of the greatest opportunities to have a larger impact with my position with the Fellowship of Christian Athletes, but it required our family to move from Virginia to Kansas City. The opportunity felt more like a curse than a blessing, because our entire family lived in Virginia. We had grown up and lived in Virginia where we had our entire community of friends and relatives. We knew no one in Kansas City. Our kids were in grade school, and they were extremely close to all their cousins. We had a great setup—ate weekly family meals, attended the same church and the same school, and even took family vacations together. Need I say more?

God was stretching us. He wanted us to leave the familiar, the safe, and the comfortable. I felt exactly like Abraham did in Genesis 12 when God asked Abraham to simply "go!"

The Lord said to Abram: Go out from your land, your relatives, and your father's house to the land that I will show you.
–Genesis 12:1 HCSB

The only advantage I had over Abraham was that I knew where I was to go: Kansas City. God just said to Abraham, "I will show you." And we find out in Genesis 12:4, "So Abram went." He obeyed because he had rubber band faith. And we did the same thing as a family. Even though it was the hardest decision we have ever made as a family, it has been the most rewarding. God blessed us when we were willing to be stretched.

As fathers and sons, we've been blessed with skills and strengths to serve and lead. It's sometimes hard to have rubber band faith, because we rely too much on our own strength and play it safe. We need to step out and ask the Lord to stretch us in all areas of our life—spiritually, physically, emotionally, mentally, financially, and relationally. When you have rubber band faith, you will immediately respond, "God did it!" When you depend on your abilities, you will respond, "I did it!"

True faith begins when it gets stretched. It starts at the edge of your comfort zone. God is waiting for fathers and sons to be bold and courageous. You are made to be stretched. Once you experience this type of faith, you'll never look back. It will be hard to imagine life without rubber band faith.

TAKE ACTION

1. Ask each other to describe rubber band faith.

2. What is the opposite of rubber band faith?

3. When has your faith been stretched the most? What were the circumstances? How did God show up?

4. Read Mark 6:4–6 together. Why was Jesus astonished? What can you learn from this passage?

5. How can rubber band faith impact your life? How can it impact your relationship with each other?

Lord God in Heaven, I ask for rubber band faith—the kind of faith that depends on You showing up. Help us to be a father and a son who live with great faith. Today, I am asking You to stretch and strengthen my faith. In the name of Jesus I pray, amen.

11

Me Monster

It's not about you.

Let another praise you, and not your own mouth; some-one else, and not your own lips.
–Proverbs 27:2 ESV

My all-time favorite comedian is Brian Regan. He is funny and clean—a hard combination to find these days. In one of his routines, he talks about running into a "Me Monster," a guy he doesn't even know who is doing all the talking for everyone else and trying to top everyone's story. It's funny and convicting.

> Beware of the Me Monster.

Identifying Me Monsters is easy because they're completely consumed with themselves. Once you've met one, you will never forget one. Me Monsters are everywhere. They lurk in sports, in schools, in businesses, in communities, and even in families.

There are three characteristics all Me Monsters have in common:

1. They are self-absorbed.
2. They care more about themselves than others.
3. They have no self-awareness.

The first full-blown Me Monster I met was a teammate on my college lacrosse team. He was excited after a tough loss just because he scored his goals. His excitement about how well he played and what he did on the field as an individual was vividly evident, regardless of the team's performance. On the other hand, if we won a big game and he didn't score or play well, he would be visibly upset in the locker room. I never saw him celebrate another teammate's success. He had all three Me Monster characteristics.

He had incredible skills as a lacrosse player. He had moves, dodges, and a shot I could only dream of having. However, because of his pursuit of self, he was not a great player. He wasn't even a good player. He was a dangerous player who damaged team chemistry and interfered with teamwork, trust, and loyalty. He lived by the me-over-we philosophy.

The part that bothered me most was not that he was on the team (I actually got to know him quite well and we had many great conversations), but that he had great skills that I didn't. It bugged me that I had the same selfish drive as him, but it was hidden in my heart. Over time, I started to see that I was just like him but I kept it secret. I was consumed with my own play, not wanting to celebrate other players doing well, and wanting all the glory. He just let it all hang out because he didn't care what others thought. What you saw was what you got. As a Christian, I couldn't let my Me Monster be seen, so I controlled it and it lurked below the surface. That made me worse than a Me Monster; it made me a hypocritical Me Monster.

God taught me a lot through this relationship. The Lord began to work on my heart and revealed to me what needed to change. I learned that, on average, we speak more than nine million words a year and that half of them are *I, me, my,* and *mine.* I was sick of focusing on me. My Me Monster teammate was a spark in my life that helped me refocus and die to the Me Monster in me.

In Mark 10, we read Jesus' conversation with a rich man that revealed the Me Monster in the man. He came to Jesus and asked him what he needed to do to inherit eternal life. Jesus referred to keeping the commandments to make the point that it would be impossible to be perfect. Interestingly, the man actually thought that he could meet that standard. So then Jesus got right down to the heart of the matter.

> Looking at the man, Jesus felt genuine love for him. "There is still one thing you haven't done," he told him. "Go and sell all your possessions and give the money to the poor, and you will have treasure in heaven. Then come, follow me." At this the man's face fell, and he went away sad, for he had many possessions. —Mark 10:21–22

This man was a Me Monster who liked having a lot of stuff. He didn't want to share it with others who had need. He didn't want to give anything away. It made him feel good to be better than others. He wanted to stand out instead of serve. Jesus constantly reminds us all that it's not about us.

There are three ways to kill the Me Monster:

1. Celebrate others' success.
2. Pray for others.
3. Serve others.

Men, we have too much pride and not enough humility. We have too much selfishness and not enough serving. We have too much self-promotion and not enough celebrating others. We must be committed to celebrating the successes of others regardless of our own success. We must be committed to always pray for others. It's hard to be a Me Monster when we are lifting others up in prayer.

This might sound crazy, but I pray that God will put a Me Monster in your life so that you can watch and learn. If you are a full-blown Me Monster, I pray that God will open your eyes so that you might see the truth about yourself. It may be time to do some soul searching and be honest with yourself.

There are Me Monsters everywhere, but the Me Monster lurks in all of us. We need to kill the Me Monster daily. The apostle Paul reminds us in Galatians 2:20 that we need to be crucified to self so that Christ can live in us and through us.

Fathers and sons, remember, it's not about you. Our lives are meant to be lived for others. Give each other permission to call each other out when the Me Monster behavior surfaces. A simple "Hey Dad, you're acting like a Me Monster" will quickly ground you and help you stop trying to impress everyone. Men, beware of the Me Monster and remember: it's not about you.

TAKE ACTION

1. Do you know a Me Monster? How did that person make you feel? How did you respond to him or her?

2. What can you learn from Me Monsters?

3. Why is it so easy for others to see what we cannot see ourselves?

4. How can you keep each other from becoming Me Monsters?

Jesus, I know it's easy to identify others as Me Monsters. It's easy to see others' gaps, weaknesses, and sins. Lord, forgive me for judging others. Help me to see the junk in my own life. Reveal to me the pride and selfishness deep in my heart that no one sees. Heal me of my pursuit of self and teach me how to die to myself every day. My desire is to praise You. You are the Famous One, not me. Today, I give You all the glory. In Jesus' name, amen.

12

PLAYTIME

CALLED TO GREATNESS PRINCIPLE
Play together; stay together.

I was raised in the greatest of homes...just a really great dad, and I miss him so much. He was a good man, very faithful, always loved my mom, always provided for the kids, and just a lot of fun.

–Max Lucado

In our family, we go to great lengths to make things fun. You might say fun is one of our core values. We were recently at the neighborhood pool, and it was absolutely packed with kids just having a blast. They turned everything into a game. Kids were flying off diving boards and sliding down the water slide. Others were playing sharks-and-minnows or racing and playing tag.

Interestingly, there were very few adults in the pool. But for forty-five minutes I took full advantage of my time with the kids—it was playtime. Then the lifeguards blew their whistles signifying adult-only swim, a fifteen-minute break with no kids in the water once every hour. For me, that whistle signified the end of fun. Kids in the water—tons of fun! No kids—no fun! I was left with only two or three other adults and then joined by all the "mature" older adults. What a bummer.

> Families that play together, stay together.

Some may say that's pretty simplistic, and obviously playing is not going to keep you together by itself, but I believe it's a key ingredient to a strong family. Playtime creates fond memories; it fosters creativity and the use of your imagination. And, perhaps best of all, it helps eliminate the isolation caused by the epidemic of personal technology. Playtime gets your face out of the iPhone, iPad, or computer screen and makes you actually engage with each other.

Playtime is a key ingredient that creates strong, lasting bonds between fathers and sons. When the kids were little, every single night when I got home from work, I was greeted with this simple statement: "Daddy, let's play!" Oh, how I loved the sound of that.

One year for my son's birthday, we created a football field in our yard with lines and everything. All his friends came over, put on flags, and divided up into the teams. I was all-time quarterback. Just as the game started, it began to downpour. Instead of pausing the game and running for cover, we made it into the best flag football memory ever. And we turned our yard into a muddy mess. We still laugh about that today. The grass didn't hold up for very long, but the memories will last a lifetime.

I believe that God created fun, play, recreation, laughter, and celebration. In John 10:10b NIV, Jesus said, "I have come that they may have life, and have it to the full." Full, abundant life is not meant just for the young. It's for everybody. Celebrations in Jesus' day were common. His first miracle was performed at a wedding celebration. Now something tells me that was a place filled with fun.

I also believe God has a tremendous sense of humor. Just take a look at some of the wacky animals he created and you'll get a good laugh. He even designed our bodies to respond to play by producing healthy hormones when we laugh; they're called endorphins, and they bring a sense of well-being, healing, and pain relief. Laughter decreases stress, boosts the immune system, lowers blood pressure, and is a natural anti-depressant. That's good news!

A cheerful heart is good medicine. –Proverbs 17:22a

Playing almost always leads to laughter, laughter brings us together, and laughter is contagious. People laugh thirty times more often when with others than they do alone. We love to be around fun people; it attracts us, doesn't it? It's also almost impossible to be mad at someone when you are playing, laughing, and having fun.

Unfortunately, as many of us get older, we get more serious and stop playtime. It becomes all about work. Life seems to wear on us as we age. Somewhere along the way people stop having fun and take everything too seriously. But in Genesis 21:5–6 NIV, Sarah reminds us that we're never too old to laugh. She even named her son Isaac, which means "laughter." He was a constant reminder of the joyful, unexpected, do-the-impossible nature of God:

Abraham was a hundred years old when his son Isaac was born to him. Sarah said, "God has brought me laughter, and everyone who hears about this will laugh with me."

Solomon shares this wisdom in Ecclesiastes 3:1, 4.

For everything there is a season, a time for every activity under heaven.... A time to cry and a time to laugh. A time to grieve and a time to dance.

I've come to realize the value of playtime even more as we've all gotten older. Tickle fights, hide-and-seek, and wrestling have been replaced by go-karts, rocket launches, and tubing. Playgrounds, flashlight tag, and capture the flag have been replaced by corn hole, pool games, and board games. But no matter what playtime is for you, it's important to make things fun.

> If you have fun being there, people have
> fun being around you. —Lou Holtz

Dads, find ways to have playtime with your sons. Be intentional about it. Get in the game and stop watching from the sidelines. Don't take yourself so seriously; be willing to laugh at yourself too. Make joyful connection the goal instead of competition. Sons, find ways to play with your dad. Find activities that you both enjoy and then do them. Turn off the television and personal technology and go play; get outside and make some memories. Life is not meant to be a spectator sport. It's meant to be played. When you play together, you stay together.

TAKE ACTION

1. Think about the things you have done together where you've played and had the most fun. Describe those times.

2. What are the biggest distractions that are keeping us from playing together? Talk these through.

3. Read John 10:10 and commit it to memory. How does fun and laughter help make life full?

4. Pick your top three "games" and put them on the calendar.

Father, thank You for the gift of playtime. Thank You for fun, laughter, and joy. We trust that You invented the idea of fun and celebration, and we ask that You would bring us a spirit of laughter and joy. Bond our hearts, minds, and spirits together as we find ways to play. Amen.

13

Show Up

CALLED TO GREATNESS PRINCIPLE
Show up or you'll miss out

No matter how you feel, get up, gear up, and show up.
–Jimmy Page

I recently had a conversation with a close friend, and he told me about a time when he came home from work following a couple of grueling weeks of training camp (he's an NFL coach, so he often leaves early and gets home late). Just as he plopped down on the couch, his son popped in and said "Dad, let's go out and shoot." Like every great dad, he got up, geared up, and showed up. I have experienced this countless times, and I've never once regretted showing up.

A couple of years ago, I encouraged my youngest son to go to a Fellowship of Christian Athletes sports camp at Kutztown University in Pennsylvania. Every year I see how God moves in the lives of young people and changes their life's direction and eternal destination. I believed this would be a life-changing experience for my son, but he didn't feel like going. He was enjoying his summer off, sleeping in and playing games, but I finally convinced him to go. To hear him talk about lessons learned and how he loved that camp made me know it was worth it. He showed up.

The examples of the blessing that comes from simply showing up are countless:

- Go to church? Didn't feel like it, but that testimony has inspired me to be better.
- Ride bikes with dad? Didn't feel like it, but hearing stories from when he was my age was priceless.
- Try out for that team? Didn't feel like it, but now I've got a band of brothers for life.

Showing up is really all about relationships. It's about connections and conversations. It's about making memories. And it's also about doing what God is asking you to do and fulfilling His purpose and plans for your life. But if you don't show up, you'll miss out. I guarantee it.

As boys grow into men and men get older, we have a tendency to withdraw, become passive, and get more isolated over time. It's easier to just stay on the sidelines, but you'll pay a high price for sitting it out. There is no substitute for your presence. God is imploring us as fathers and sons to engage, to get involved, and to show up.

In the Bible, God uses Moses as an illustration of his desire for His people to show up when He asks us to. God had heard the cries of His people who suffered in slavery under the oppressive hand of the Egyptians for four hundred years; He was going to set them free and lead them to the Promised Land. When God spoke to Moses at the burning bush, he asked Moses to show up on behalf of God's people and confront Pharaoh. He called Moses by name and said,

> Now go, for I am sending you to Pharaoh. You must lead my people Israel out of Egypt. —Exodus 3:10

All Moses really had to do was show up and deliver the message; God was going to do the rest for His glory. But Moses wanted nothing to do with it. He went passive and started to make excuses. He tried to get out of it five separate times:

1. **He said, "Who am I?"**
   "But Moses protested to God, 'Who am I to appear before Pharaoh? Who am I to lead the people of Israel out of Egypt?'" Exodus 3:11.

2. **He said, "Who are You?"**
   "But Moses protested, 'If I go to the people of Israel and tell them, 'The God of your ancestors has sent me to you,' they will ask me, 'What is his name?' Then what should I tell them?'" Exodus 3:13.

3. **He said, "It won't work."**
   "But Moses protested again, 'What if they won't believe me or listen to me? What if they say, 'The LORD never appeared to you'?" Exodus 4:1.

4. **He said, "I'm not good enough."**
   "But Moses pleaded with the LORD, 'O Lord, I'm not very good with words. I never have been, and I'm not now, even though you have spoken to me. I get tongue-tied, and my words get tangled'" Exodus 4:10.

5. **He finally just said, "Anybody but me!"**
   "But Moses again pleaded, 'Lord, please! Send anyone else'" Exodus 4:13.

God had something big planned for Moses, and Moses didn't want to show up for God. I believe the same is especially true for fathers and sons. We have an enemy that does not want us to show up; he wants to separate us. He loves to distract, divide, and defeat us.

The thief's purpose is to "steal and kill and destroy" (John 10:10a). And he appeals to the fact that the easy road is always so attractive to us. We desire comfort and convenience, and most of us don't like conflict.

> Great things never come from comfort zones.

The Enemy does not want you to show up. He will do everything he can to get in the way of what God is trying to do in your heart, relationships, and life. He wants to disrupt what God wants to do through you to bless others.

> Stay alert! Watch out for your great enemy, the devil. He prowls around like a roaring lion, looking for someone to devour. –1 Peter 5:8

He wants to keep you out of the game on the sidelines. He'll make you super busy. He'll distract you. He'll remind you how tired you are. He'll make something else seem more exciting. He'll create conflict if he can—and on and on it goes. He wants to make us feel inadequate, unworthy, and out of place.

> We need to step out before we find out.

Fathers and sons, we need to take a step of faith and rely on God's power to do the miraculous. If we don't step out in obedience, we'll never find out what God has in store.

So fathers, show up for your sons even if you're tired. And sons, show up for your dads even if you have something else you want to do. It will be worth it. God does his best work when you're together.

And both of you need to show up for God and do what He asks you to do even if you don't think you're the right man for the job. Show up or you'll miss out.

TAKE ACTION

1. Why is it so important that fathers and sons show up for each other?

2. Talk about a time when you decided not to show up and what you missed out on.

3. Talk about times you have showed up and the blessing that came from it. Put another activity on your calendar right now.

Father, thank You that You want to do the miraculous in our relationship and through us and that all You ask is that we show up. Help us to desire time together and take advantage of big and small opportunities to be together. Help us hear Your voice and be available when You call our name. Amen.

14

FIVE PURITY PRINCIPLES

CALLED TO GREATNESS PRINCIPLE
Purity paves the way to intimacy.

Who is pure of heart? Only those who have surrendered their hearts completely to Jesus that He may reign in them alone.

—Dietrich Bonhoeffer

Each year I go through the process of discovering my "One Word" for the year that guides me and refines me. This One Word vision, year after year, gives me the focus I need to pursue God's best, maintain mission and meaning, and live with power and purpose.

Several years ago, the Lord revealed the word *Pure* to me as my word for the year. The funny thing was that whenever I shared my word with others, I received the same response: silence, blank stares, and awkward conversation. How would you expect someone to respond to that word? "Good for you"; "You need it"; "Glad it's your word, not mine"; or just, "I'll be praying for you." Even though it was awkward to tell people my word, it was a powerful year of discovering the depths of purity.

Everyone thinks purity deals with one thing only: physical

purity. And yes, that is a huge issue that every man struggles with at one time or another. It's important that fathers and sons talk openly and honestly about the physical struggle that so many men never discuss. Too much is at stake for fathers and sons not to have total transparency to pursue physical purity. When my son was thirteen, we had a Purity Weekend where we went away to talk with total transparency about physical purity. Thanks to the ministry Family Life and their resource, the Passport2Purity Getaway Kit, we were able to structure an unforgettable weekend to talk about issues that I otherwise would never have felt comfortable discussing.

However, physical purity is only the tip of the iceberg. Developing a pure life stretches beyond the sexual dimension. Purity pertains to every area of life—mind, body, and spirit. It is revealed in our thoughts, words, attitudes, motives, and actions. And all of these things are reflections of the condition of our heart; everything flows from there.

> Guard your heart above all else, for it determines the course of your life. –Proverbs 4:23

How we guard our heart is key. What we see, say, hear, and do will either protect or pollute our heart. Guarding your heart is done in three specific tangible ways, all found in Proverbs 4:23–27.

1. **Guard your eyes.**
   Access to pictures, videos, Internet, TV, and images on social media will affect your heart. If those inputs (like sexual images and immoral behaviors) are bringing impurity, your heart will be polluted. We need to safeguard and protect what we allow our eyes to see. Keep your eyes on Jesus and His path of purity for you.

2. **Guard your ears.**
   Messages from the media found in music and other outlets will either build you up or bring you down. Those repetitive negative or toxic messages will make you sick. Listening to positive or godly messages and lyrics will lift your heart.

3. **Guard your steps.**
   The places you go and the things you experience there also affect your heart. Using God's Word as a lamp and light will keep you on His path in His footsteps. Be careful about the places you go. Friends can have a big influence here as well, so choose them wisely.

Purity positively impacts our relationships, emotions, and spiritual life. But impurity has a negative impact. It weighs us down with guilt and shame and makes us timid and passive. It distracts us from God's best path and direction for our lives. We cannot afford to be weakened by the burden of sin and derailed from His purpose in our lives.

God desires for us to be pure for His glory, not our gain. There are amazing blessings and benefits when we pursue purity—like a clear conscience, clean hands, and close relationships—but they're not the primary goal. We pursue purity so that our lives can glorify God and ultimately please Him in all we do. As a result, we will experience God in a more rich and powerful way. Why purity? Jesus answered that in eleven words:

> Blessed are the pure in heart, for they will see God.
> –Matthew 5:8 NIV

A life of purity is produced from a life marked with brokenness, surrender, and sacrifice; this is the road less traveled. Purity is a way of life when we hide God's Word in our heart. Purity has two close friends who stand on each side of it: holiness and righteousness. These are results of our pursuit of Christ.

Here are five principles that God revealed to me during my year-long experience with purity:

1. **Purity ignites intimacy.**
   This is true with our relationship with Jesus and others. Fellowship with God demands purity. Sins like unresolved conflict, jealousy, or pride create separation and distance. But purity of heart paves the way to transparent, authentic relationships. Seeking God's forgiveness regularly helps maintain purity.

2. **Purity precedes power.**
   There is spiritual power that flows from purity. Purity comes from a spirit of humility. God's power is made perfect in our weakness. We become God's clear channel of strength and courage when purity paves the way. When we lack purity, we lack spiritual confidence.

3. **Purity leads to simplicity.**
   Sin brings problems and complexity to our lives. However, a life of purity is marked with integrity, which brings simplicity. There is nothing more complicated than carrying around small compromises and secrets and having to cover up your tracks.

   Whoever walks in integrity walks securely, but whoever takes crooked paths will be found out. –Proverbs 10:9 NIV

4. **Purity cultivates peace.**
   Sin results in unrest, but purity results in joy. It's hard to be at peace when you're worried about someone

discovering that the *real you* is not the *you* they thought they knew. Purity creates a what-you-see-is-what-you-get sense of peace.

5. **Purity brings freedom.**
   We discover freedom from guilt and sin when purity is at the core. Too many people are enslaved and entangled in their sin. Because of Jesus, we are free—free indeed!

   So if the Son sets you free, you will be free indeed.
   –John 8:36 NIV

Fathers and sons, pursue purity at all costs. When you struggle and fail, come clean quickly. Confess your struggle to each other and to God. Your family's legacy is counting on it. Have the talk. Punch awkward in the face and put everything on the table. Create a no-condemnation environment (Romans 8:1–2). Let God do the revealing and convicting. Purity always paves the way to intimacy.

TAKE ACTION

1. Are you experiencing victorious living when it comes to purity? Why or why not?

2. What principle hits home the most? Why?

3. What are the things that keep you from a life of purity?

4. Have the talk. Create common ground. Allow the Holy Spirit to lead.

Father God, help me to be pure in all areas of life. I want to have intimacy in all my relationships, and first starting with You. When I pursue purity, it glorifies You. And pursing purity allows me to know You, Lord. In Jesus' name, amen.

15

Two Ounces
of Power

CALLED TO GREATNESS PRINCIPLE
The heart controls the tongue.

And a small rudder makes a huge ship turn wherever the pilot chooses to go, even though the winds are strong. In the same way, the tongue is a small thing that makes grand speeches. But a tiny spark can set a great forest on fire.

–James 3:4–5

When I was sixteen years old, I was felt confident and cocky. My head was big because of the pride in my heart. Athletic success, the right friends, and popularity made me feel invincible. I had a full-blown ego that caused me to think I could do or say anything I wanted, but that all came crashing down one afternoon when I had a disagreement with my mother. I can't even remember what the argument was about, but I do remember what I said that ended the discussion.

I blurted a horrible, painful, cutting sentence that destroyed her. She broke down...and I mean broke down. One sentence heard around the world! At the time, I had no idea how or why I said it. However, I know now that it came from a heart that wasn't right. My heart was controlling my tongue and it simply slipped out under pressure. I am thankful for a godly mom who forgave me, and we now look back at that encounter as a defining moment in getting my heart realigned.

> The most powerful two ounces of body weight
> we possess are found in the tongue.

It has been said that the tongue weighs practically nothing, yet very few people can contain its power. The average human tongue weighs only two ounces, but it is considered one of the strongest muscles in the body. The tongue is a tough worker. Like the heart, it is always working—helping mix food, forming letters and sounds, and filtering out germs. Even while we sleep it constantly pushes saliva down our throats. It never rests. I know this isn't biology class, but the tongue is an amazing part of our body, and it reveals more about a person's spiritual life than anything else. Truly, the tongue is the window to the soul.

The average person will have thirty conversations a day and produce about sixteen thousand words. In one year, your words would fill 132 books with 400 pages in each. You will spend roughly 20 percent of your life yakking away. Where does the tongue get its incredible power? From the heart. There is a Scottish proverb that says, "When the heart is full, the tongue will speak." Often, people will utter something and then quickly say, "I didn't mean that." Actually, they probably meant it; they just didn't mean to *say* it. We mean everything we say, but we often don't plan to allow our tongues to expose our hearts.

> The tongue is the only tool that gets sharper with use.
> —Washington Irving

If there is hatred in a person's heart, the tongue will spew criticism. Fear in the heart will bring negative words. An impure heart will produce foul speech. An undisciplined heart will result in sloppy language. Hurtful words will come from a wounded heart. But, conversely, if there is joy in a heart, encouragement will flow from the tongue. A peaceful heart will result in words of hope. Words of blessing will come from a secure heart. An honest heart will reveal a heart full of truth. In essence, the true key to controlling your tongue really is an issue of the heart.

Most fathers and sons struggle with their mouths. Our tongues slip because they live in a wet place. The book of James compares the tongue to fire because of the potential damage it can inflict. It's interesting how it is compared to fire and not water. A small glass of water wouldn't likely start a flood, but one small careless spark can destroy thousands of acres. The tongue has the same potential, and James warns us that the tongue can pollute our whole body.

James 3:8 NIV says, "but no human being can tame the tongue. It is a restless evil, full of deadly poison." The truth is that we can't control it, but God can. We need to allow Him to take hold of our tongues and cleanse them. We've heard the saying, "What's wrong? Cat got your tongue?" Well, maybe we should pray to be asked, "What's wrong? God got your tongue?"

Fathers, your words can bring daily blessing or curses to your sons. The choice is yours—life or death. Sons, with so many young people spilling out garbage from their mouths, you can be the one who accentuates the positive with your words. Every day my son hears words of blessing, encouragement, and positivity from me. I will not let a day go by that he doesn't hear life-giving words from his father.

Ask God to control your tongue by purifying your heart. Understand that your words will either bring healing or hurt, blessings or burdens, truth or torture. Let others know you as someone who has a tame tongue that speaks truth and life with two small ounces of power.

TAKE ACTION

1. The goal is to bring blessing, life, and encouragement with your tongue for a twenty-four-hour period. Fathers and sons, for just one day, focus on the positive. Carry a three-by-five card with you. If you say anything critical, negative, or condemning, write it down on one side of the card. If you say anything positive or encouraging, write it down on the other side. At the end of the day, review what you said and why you said it.

2. Have you said something hurtful that seemed as if it came out of nowhere? What did you learn from it?

3. Why do you think it is so hard to control the tongue?

4. When is it the hardest for you to speak life? When is it the easiest?

5. What is one tangible way that you can remind each other about the power and purpose of your words?

Father, thank You for the power of our words. I confess that, on my own, I can't control my tongue and often use it to speak negative words and destruction. Still, I desire to accentuate the positive. I want my words to bring life and deliver Your truth, but it is so hard to control my tongue. First, please touch my heart. Cleanse it and purify it. Make my heart right so that love spills out of my mouth. Then, may these two ounces of power be used for Your glory. In the name of Jesus I pray, amen.

16

ONE WORD

Focus gives power to your purpose.

Resolutions are about what you want to get done; One Word is about who you will become.

–Jon Gordon, Dan Britton & Jimmy Page

When my oldest son was getting ready to head off to college, he was struggling with a decision about whether he should try out for his college lacrosse team. The coach had invited him to come out in the fall and compete for a position, but he wasn't sure he was going to do it. He'd had a good high school experience, but I sensed that he may have been lacking confidence and needed some encouragement. I knew exactly what he was going through because I'd had a similar experience with college baseball.

I told him my story and shared the sense of regret that I had for not going for it when I had my opportunity. I then asked him what his One Word was for that year and he said, "Boom." I laughed because I knew it was just what he needed at this very moment. He believed this year would be a breakthrough year where he would go for it, take risks, and come into his own. This was a perfect opportunity to live out his word. I knew that no matter how it turned out, by living out his word *Boom*, God would remind him of His presence, purpose, and power in his life. He decided to go for it, made the team, and can live without regret.

Every year for almost twenty years, we've been discovering our One Word themes for the year. We used to make New Year's resolutions, but encountered frustration and failure, just like everybody else. We started with good intentions but finished the year in virtually the same place we started. Resolutions are about *what* you hope to get done; One Word is about *who* you want to become.

But by narrowing the focus to just One Word, we have discovered the secret to life change. Less is best. The simplicity of focusing on One Word for the year brings clarity, power, and passion. It provides a filter and a focus for the year and helps us restore mission and meaning to our everyday lives. One Word is the secret to focusing on what matters most, and this focus gives power to our purpose.

Paul understood the power of focus. In Philippians 3, he pioneered the idea of focusing on one thing:

> But one thing I do: Forgetting what is behind and straining toward what is ahead, I press on toward the goal to win the prize for which God has called me heavenward in Christ Jesus. –Phil 3:13–14 NIV

He put his past behind him and pressed on with focus. Narrowing the focus allows us to keep our eyes on the prize, finish the race, and receive the reward.

Jesus modeled the power of focus as well. He did exactly

what the Father asked Him to do. He was never in a hurry and never controlled by the desires of the crowd. He was on a mission and would not be distracted or derailed along the way.

The One Word process has three simple steps: *look in, look up,* and *look out.*

1. Look In –Prepare Your Heart

This is where you take action to unplug from the hectic pace, noise, and clutter. Finding solitude and silence can be a difficult task, but hearing from God is essential. There are three key questions to ask God as you look in: What do I need? What's in my way? What needs to go?

2. Look Up –Discover Your Word

This step helps us plug in and listen to God. We believe that God has a word that is meant for you. Taking time for prayer is the place to start. Ask Him this question: What do You want to do in me and through me this year? This question will help you discover the word meant for you.

3. Look Out –Live Your Word

Once you discover the word that is meant for you, it's time to live it out. Keep your One Word front and center. Tell your inner circle of friends and your family. Write it in your journal. Post it on your refrigerator. Paint a One Word picture and hang it up where you will see it every day. Talk about it with your family at the dinner table. Do whatever it takes to keep it in focus and keep it fresh.

One Word has been a life-changing journey for my boys and me. Each son can look back on past words and remember how God used them in his life. One year, my middle son's word was *Do*. He developed a get-it-done mind-set of taking action. He started to get better at seeing what needed to be done and stepping up. Procrastination became a thing of the past. He has carried that life change forward and is known as someone who can be counted on to just *Do* it.

A couple of years ago, my youngest son chose *Today*. He had just made the transition to middle school and was increasingly anxious and stressed out about everything he had to do. He felt weighed down and like he was missing out on good things along the way. The stress was stealing his joy. *Today* helped him focus on one day and one thing at a time. It helped him in his academic and spiritual life. He was able to enjoy the present more and stop worrying about the future so much.

As a dad, I can look back on how each word has helped shape me more and more into the likeness of Christ. It has been a challenging process, but so rewarding. Knowing and seeing how God is using it in my boys helps me see progress and remember that God loves them even more than I do.

One Word is a family tradition that has changed our entire family. It has impacted every area of life—spiritual, mental, emotional, relational, physical, and even financial. One Word will change the way you think, the words you speak, the attitudes of your heart, your relationships, and even your actions. Every year we have experienced God's use of our One Word to write a chapter of His story in our lives full of milestones and memories. It has changed who we are.

As fathers and sons, discover your One Word and begin to live it out. You will gain insight into what God is doing in your life. It provides many opportunities to encourage each other along the road of transformation. One Word provides the focus needed to give power to your purpose.

TAKE ACTION

1. Go through the One Word process together to discover your One Word for the year.

2. Share your One Word and discuss the reasons why you chose it.

3. Take action to put your One Word front and center as a reminder and revisit progress each week.

Father, thank You for the power of focus through One Word. Help us to use this tool to live with more clarity, power, and purpose. Bring our hearts together and help us encourage each other to become everything God has made us to be. Amen.

TWENTY QUESTIONS

CALLED TO GREATNESS PRINCIPLE
Always ask.

You do not have because you do not ask God.

—James 4:2 NIV

ave you ever played the game Twenty Questions? One person thinks of an answer and the others get to ask twenty questions in an effort to figure it out; they use each question to narrow it down until they are confident they can guess the right answer. It's a fun game that challenges the guessers to ask really good questions or they will never get the right answer. One thing is for sure—the guessers never leave any questions un-asked. If you need them, you ask all twenty questions before making your final guess. We used to play this game on long car rides to pass the time and satisfy our competitive nature.

That game made me good at asking questions, especially when it came to asking for something that I really wanted. So when I went to my parents and said, "Can I ask you a question?" they always responded with, "It never hurts to ask." Now I learned quickly that it didn't mean I would always get what I wanted, but I also learned a valuable lesson—always ask. Never assume that the answer will be no; never answer for someone else by not asking.

We remind our sons, "Never say no for someone else." For some reason, we love to say no for others. Remember, you miss all the shots you don't have the courage to take. The worst thing that can happen is that you get a no. But when you ask, you leave the possibility for a yes. I have passed this lesson on.

In the movie *Evan Almighty*, Morgan Freeman plays the character of God. In one scene, Freeman is having a conversation with Evan's wife, and he poses the very same question in three different ways:

- If you ask for patience, does God give you patience or does He give you opportunities to be patient?
- If you ask for courage, does God give you courage or does He give you opportunities to be courageous?
- If you ask for a close family, does God zap you with warm, fuzzy feelings or does He give you opportunities to love each other?

> God doesn't always give us exactly what we want.

Fortunately, God loves us too much to give us everything we want at the very moment we want it. Instead of fixing our circumstances instantly, He often puts us on a journey to develop something in us and not just to fix something for us. God cares more about the fruit that is being produced in us and through us than about providing a simple solution; He cares more about our character than our circumstances. There is more power in the process than the outcome, and there is more to be learned on the journey than at the destination.

Sometimes when we ask God for something, He answers in unexpected ways. We often want the answer to be easy, comfortable, and safe. We want God to just give us what we ask for. This is how we must sound to God: "Can you just fix my problems? Can you make me popular? Or give me good grades? Can you help me make the team? Can I just wake up in the morning with everything going my way?" Even though our questions may sometimes seem silly, God says, "Always ask."

Keep on asking.

As a father, I love saying yes when my boys ask me for something, but sometimes I've found it's better to say no or tell them to wait. Since I always have what's best in mind for my boys, and I keep an eye on their character and their future, I try to apply wisdom when I answer. Sometimes saying yes would be the worst possible answer. It's the same with God our Father. He doesn't always give us what we want now, but He does give us what we need most. Sometimes that means we go through challenges that test our faith and humble us. Sometimes the answer seems to take a long time to get here and we grow tired of asking. Don't say no for God. Just keep on asking.

Keep on asking, and you will receive what you ask for. Keep on seeking, and you will find. Keep on knocking, and the door will be opened to you. For everyone who asks, receives. Everyone who seeks, finds. And to everyone who knocks, the door will be opened. You parents—if your children ask for a loaf of bread, do you give them a stone instead? Or if they ask for a fish, do you give them a snake? Of course not! So if you sinful people know how to give good gifts to your children, how much more will your heavenly Father give good gifts to those who ask him. –Matthew 7:7–11

When we get in the habit of going to God for little things, we eventually trust Him for the bigger, more meaningful things. He tells us to ask for these things: wisdom, protection, provision, and direction. God loves to give good gifts to His kids. He always knows what's best for us and doesn't want us to settle for less than His best.

Ask for patience, and then get ready to face circumstances that will test your patience. Ask for courage, and then get ready to face circumstances beyond your capabilities. Ask for a loving family, and then get ready to be intentional about expressing love when given the opportunity. Ask for wisdom, and then get ready to be faced with choices that require you to seek God for direction. But no matter what—always ask. God will be faithful to give you good gifts that are exactly what you need.

So remember…always ask.

TAKE ACTION

1. Do you ever feel that the things you ask God for are small or unimportant?

2. What are some things you might ask God for that are important to you and God? Read James 1:5–6 and Matthew 6:9–13.

3. Read 1 John 5:14–15. What does this passage tell us about what we should be asking for? How do we know if the things we are asking God for are pleasing to Him?

4. Over the next week, write down a list of three questions you want to ask your dad. And dads, answer those questions to give your sons insight into the things that have made you into the person you are today.

Father, thank You for telling us to come to You and ask for whatever we need, just like a child asks a parent. We trust that You know exactly what we need when we need it. Help us to listen carefully for Your answers. Amen.

18

RELENTLESS

CALLED TO GREATNESS PRINCIPLE
The relentless take ground.

*But we are not those who draw back and are destroyed,
but those who have faith and obtain life.*

–Hebrews 10:39 HCSB

When I was growing up, my dad always said, "Work hard. Play hard." We sure worked hard, but I don't remember playing hard. Usually the work time took up the playtime. When we did work around the house (usually every Saturday for hours), he loved to have goals, and we pursued them with everything we had. Nothing got in our way. We gave our all—all the time. We did not give up or give in. And we never gave out. My dad's middle name should have been *Relentless*.

> It's hard to beat relentless.
> –Jay Bilas

It seems as if *relentless* is everywhere these days. There is a Relentless energy drink, Relentless Nike running shoes, *Relentless* movie, "Relentless" country album, and even a Relentless steak and lobster restaurant. If you had to define *relentless* in one word, what word would you choose? There are several good one-word definitions that I've found in dictionaries and thesauruses: unyielding, unbending, determined, never-ceasing, persistent.

As we unpack the concept of being relentless, it's good to look at it many different ways. The opposite of relentless is "to relent." Here are some one-word definitions of *relent*: abandon, soften, relax, bend, weaken. These words were not part of my dad's vocabulary. One definition of *relent* even read, "to melt or dissolve under the influence of heat."

> Relentless means to be strong.
> Relent means to be weak.

My translation of Hebrews 10:39 would be, "But we are not those who *relent*, but those who are *relentless.*" God wants us to move forward, be strong, and not give up. As followers of Christ, we need to have relentless love, pursue relentless devotion, and be on a relentless mission.

As fathers and sons, we need to be relentless—someone who has grit and guts. There is no room for fading, melting, rusting out, or burning out. We need to have tenacity and fortitude. As men, we need to reject passivity and rely on God's power in us. No more standing on the sidelines and expecting other people to step up. Relentless men don't go dark and disappear. We stand up for our faith. We take ground for the kingdom of God.

During my first week of college, a challenge by a teammate became a defining moment for me. I was one of twenty recruited freshman who were battling to earn a spot on the roster of the varsity lacrosse team. It was intense. To make matters worse, all of the freshman had the same row of lockers and the battling wasn't just on the field. I was praying I would just make the team. All of the new players looked so good and came in with so many honors and credentials.

On the third day of practice, as I was walking out of the shower with my towel on, I turned the corner and another freshman said, "Hey, I heard you're a born-again Christian. Are you?" The entire locker room went silent and all heads turned. I felt exposed, and not just because I only had a towel on. It felt as if time had stopped.

The three simple words I uttered defined who I was the next four years: "Yes, I am." I didn't try to explain what a born-again Christian was. I didn't ask him how he found out. I did not relent. It was time to make a stand for my faith. God used that moment to let the entire team know what the most important thing in my life was: my faith in Jesus Christ. Not only did I have four amazing years of ministry on the team, but I still get calls and e-mails from guys on the team (we're talking almost thirty years later) who tell me that they've come to Christ and they remember my relentless faith. They just want to thank me for being their only college example of a follower of Christ.

Relentless followers of Christ are able to absorb the inevitable criticism, obstacles, challenges, and setbacks and keep advancing. They keep their eyes on Jesus and are willing to be counted. Paul reminds us in Galatians 6:9,

> So let's not get tired of doing what is good. At just the right time we will reap a harvest of blessing if we don't give up.

Swimming upstream against the flow gets tiring. However, we will see God do great things if we don't give up. The relentless don't quit.

> Relentless men take ground
> for Christ every single day.

My goal for myself and my son is to be relentless and take ground. I desire for him not to grow tired of doing good and not to give up. Teaching him to be focused on the finish line will develop a relentless heart. My prayer is for him to always stay in step with the Holy Spirit, move forward, and take ground. Waiting for God's instruction is critical.

God loves it when His children are relentless. We become decisive, not hesitant. So the next time someone asks you how you're doing, let the answer be, "I am relentless and taking ground for Christ." Relentless fathers and sons take ground for the kingdom of God.

TAKE ACTION

1. When is it easy for you to be relentless? When is it hard?

2. Give an example of when you relented. What was the outcome?

3. In what areas are you just covering ground? Taking ground?

4. Why is it tiring doing good? Share some examples with each other. Does it change as you get older?

5. When do you feel like quitting?

6. Read Psalm 31:24. How does this verse encourage you to be relentless?

7. Together, turn Hebrews 10:39 into a Relentless Prayer. Pray this prayer for each other.

Father, teach me how to be relentless. I desire to take ground for You. Show me how to move from being busy to being strategic. I ask for Your power and might to be relentless all the time. In Jesus' name, amen.

19

FOLLOWERSHIP

CALLED TO GREATNESS PRINCIPLE
Follow well; lead well.

To be a good leader, at some point you have to be a good follower. I was always a good follower. I always followed the right people and listened to the right things. Those helped shape me as a leader.

–Chauncey Billups, NBA player

"Are you a leader or a follower?" I can't tell you how many times I heard that when I was growing up. But when adults asked me that question, I don't think they wanted an answer. As a teenager, I heard it from my youth pastor, parents, coaches, friends, and other caring individuals. A subtle principle was communicated through that question: *Be a leader, not a follower.*

But if everyone is leading, then who is following? I have never heard anyone confess, "I am just a follower. Leadership is not for me." Especially in our current recognition-hungry society, we all want to lead. Volumes have been written on leadership, but very little has been written on followership— you know, the art and skill of being a great follower. There are no articles, books, blogs, or interviews on the subject. Nada. Nothing.

Many years ago I attended a national youth summit in New Mexico with hundreds of the best youth leaders in the world. As a young leader, I was eager to learn from the leadership giants who were going to invest in us for several days. On the second day, I heard one of the keynote speakers, Dan Webster, challenge all the leaders on the concept of leadership of the heart. As he spoke, I found myself floating between conviction and motivation.

I pursued him at the summit and asked him questions about spiritual leadership. From that weekend in New Mexico, God graciously allowed us to become great friends. Now as one of my spiritual mentors in life, Dan has taught me more about leadership than anyone else. However, the most powerful thing about Dan is that he is a great follower. He is constantly studying, reading, and pursuing others to learn and grow. He is a true example of followership.

There are five powerful followership principles I have learned over the years:

1. **Followership is the beginning of leadership.**
   The best leaders have mastered the art of following, and that is why people are drawn to them. Following does not mean going with the flow and doing what everyone else is doing. Following means intentionally watching, learning from, and imitating others. You observe those who are walking in a manner worthy of the Lord, who live with humility and courage, who exhibit integrity and compassion, who make wise decisions, and then you choose to follow in their footsteps. Paul, as he followed the example of Jesus, urged other believers to imitate him.

Follow my example as I follow the example of Christ.
–1 Corinthians 11:1 NIV

You don't follow others based on title or position but on example and influence. Those you imitate will not share about all the people who follow them; instead, they'll tell of the people they follow, the lessons they've learned, and which path to take.

2. **Followership starts with humility.**
    Followers admit they don't know it all and can learn from others. They are humble. They have a thirst to grow and get better. They don't need the glory or recognition; instead, they pass on the praise to those around them. They share the love. Every day that they wake up, they clothe themselves with humility. Putting on humility needs to become a daily discipline.

    In the same way, you who are younger must accept the authority of the elders. And all of you, dress yourselves in humility as you relate to one another, for "God opposes the proud but gives grace to the humble." –1 Peter 5:5

3. **Followership grows with serving.**
    If being a great leader means being a great follower, then what is the secret to being a great follower? It's being a servant. Followers have a willingness to serve others in sacrificial, humbling ways. A leader is someone who follows Christ's example of serving.

    For even the Son of Man did not come to be served, but to serve, and to give his life as a ransom for many.
    –Mark 10:45 NIV

4. Followership is perfected with Jesus.

Jesus was the ultimate follower. He followed the voice and will of His Father. He served and sacrificed. He gave up His glory for our ultimate good. He didn't seek the spotlight or the position of power. Instead, He walked with humility and compassion. He served to give, not to get. God calls us to follow Him first and to follow Him daily:

Then he said to the crowd, "If any of you wants to be my follower, you must turn from your selfish ways, take up your cross daily, and follow me. If you try to hang on to your life, you will lose it. But if you give up your life for my sake, you will save it." –Luke 9:23–24

5. Followership begins at the foot of the cross.

Jesus never called us to be leaders, just followers. Is your goal to lead or follow? Jesus says don't lead until you follow. Jesus became the ultimate leader because He was the ultimate follower. Time to pick up your cross and follow Him.

Fathers, teach your sons that leadership starts with followership. Sons, learn now how to lead by first following. Remember, when you follow well, you lead well.

TAKE ACTION

1. How can followership change your relationship with your son/father?

2. Why is it hard to be a follower?

3. Who is a great follower that you know? What makes that person a great follower?

4. What is one way you can help each other become better followers?

Father, thank You for Your Son, Jesus Christ, who was the perfect example. I confess that on my own, I'd rather lead than follow. There is something in me that wants to be powerful and popular, not humble and serving. Please transform my heart. Teach me what it means to be a follower first. In the name of Jesus I pray, amen.

20

LOVE
WINS

You can't lose when you love.

Faith, hope, and love remain. But the greatest of these is love.

—Jesus

was speaking to a large corporate audience, and we were talking about making a difference and leaving a mark. Now most of those in this group were men who had enjoyed a lot of success over time. They were driven by the scoreboard and, in business terms, they got a lot of wins.

I challenged them on a more personal level with this simple question: "What's one word you want people to think of when they think of you?" The responses were what I expected—*driven, passionate, successful, strong, steady, leader, provider.* What I didn't expect was their response to the one word I shared—*love.* I could literally hear the jokes coming from a number of the guys as they sarcastically considered how a real man could choose the word *love.* What they were probably really thinking was, *I'm not good at that.*

But the truth is, the word I hope marks my life is *love.* I hope to leave a lot of great character qualities in the hearts of my boys, but if love isn't in the mix, I believe I will have failed them. Most men have a hard time with this because we're so confused about what it means and how to express it; we are often uncomfortable with expressing emotions other than anger or frustration. We equate love with being soft. We'd rather be warriors and winners. We'd rather be tough than tender. We generally don't think *love* is a masculine word unless it's associated with physical pleasure. We are bombarded by images that look like love, but are really just lust.

Fathers and sons need to get this right. Dads need to figure out how to love their boys so they can live up to their potential and live a life that matters. Every time I hear love described or see love demonstrated in the Bible, I am challenged by how difficult it is to love the way God wants me to love, with the right mix of compassion, kindness, and strength.

When Jesus was challenged to name the most important command, he said *love.*

> And you must love the LORD your God with all your heart, all your soul, all your mind, and all your strength. The second is equally important: "Love your neighbor as yourself."
> –Mark 12:30–31

I don't know about you, but both of these are really hard for me. I find that I get distracted by a lot of stuff and frustrated by people every now and then. Jesus later challenges us that:

> There is no greater love than to lay down one's life for one's friends. –John 15:13

That sounds like love requires an incredible amount of sacrifice. It doesn't sound weak at all. It sounds strong.

Real love never gives up, especially when times are tough.
Real love isn't jealous, proud, rude, or easily angered.
Real love sacrifices and puts other people first.
Real love doesn't keep score or bring up the past.
Real love doesn't take pleasure in other people's pain.
Real love rejoices in truth and justice.
Real love trusts God, hopes for the best, and perseveres.
Real love always defends and protects.
Real love always wins, never fails, and never ends.

Several years ago I took an assessment to discover my love language. There are five common love languages—*words*, *touch*, *quality time*, *gifts*, and *service*. Each one of us is uniquely wired with a dominant preference for how we like to experience love. We asked each of the kids to identify theirs as well so we would be better able to help them feel loved. If your son's love language is quality time and you give him gifts instead, chances are he won't feel fully loved. All love languages are good; knowing each other's helps you express love best and hit the bulls-eye of the target. It is important to know what your son's "come from" is and how to properly love him.

There are four A's of love that every son needs from his dad—*acceptance*, *affirmation*, *affection*, and *admiration*:

1. **Acceptance**
   Every boy needs to know that his dad loves him just the way God made him. Love doesn't compare. It can never be based on performance because no one will ever be perfect. Acceptance means loving our boys even when they fail or fall short, or turn their backs, and when they come back home. It means you value the things they like and try to join them in what they do.

2. **Affirmation**

   Every boy needs to hear words of affirmation from his dad. Love doesn't condemn. Encouragement around the unique gifts and talents that God has given him helps him discover his unique path and purpose in life. Speaking words of life will help your son become everything God made him to be.

3. **Affection**

   Every boy needs a physical connection with his dad. Love doesn't isolate. Physical touch prevents distance from coming between you. Roughhousing, hugs, and fist-bumps (or however you connect) go a long way, especially in public. Even the way you look at your son can communicate tenderness, kindness, and affection. Positive emotional connection is essential.

4. **Admiration**

   Every boy, especially as he becomes a young man, needs to hear and feel his dad's admiration. Love doesn't criticize. When a father begins to express admiration of his son, the son is emboldened to become everything God made him to be. When a son knows his dad admires him and is proud of him, he will live with honor and be inspired to greatness.

   Real love is not for the weak; it's for the strong. In fact, the Bible teaches us that we can have the gift of prophecy, great faith, and even give everything to the poor, but without love we are nothing and have nothing (1 Corinthians 13:2–3). Real love avoids harsh criticism, unreachable comparison, and hurtful condemnation. Can you imagine if your life together as father and son was marked by love? You would ooze humility, kindness, courage, sacrifice, honor, and strength. You would model what it looks like to stick in there when the going gets tough. You would stand up and protect your family. You would sacrifice for the good of those you love. Love always wins. You simply can't lose when you love.

TAKE ACTION

1. Take the love language profile at http://www.5love languages.com/profile/teens/. Share and discuss your love language.

2. Fill in the blank: "I feel most loved by you when _____."

3. Read 1 Corinthians 13:1–8. What aspect of love is most important to you right now? Why?

4. Discuss the four A's of love. How are you doing in each area?

Father, help us to be a father and son who love well. Help us speak each other's love language and express acceptance, affirmation, affection, and admiration. Make us into men who have the courage to love with strength, honor, and kindness. Let our lives be marked by love. Amen.

21

Turn the Light On

CALLED TO GREATNESS PRINCIPLE
Lose your light; lose your life.

Darkness is only driven out by light, not more darkness.
–Dr. Martin Luther King Jr.

Several years ago we went to the Trail West Family Camp in Buena Vista, Colorado. One of the days we decided to go on a tour through some caves and experience the underground world. We pretty much stuck to the steps and pathways that were put in place for tourists and followed our guide. The guide told stories of people who had made it through and others who had died along the way. I started to feel a little claustrophobic.

At one point the guide took us to a "room" deep within the cave and far from any natural light, and described what "real" cavers would have experienced before the caves were converted for tours. Real cavers, if they lost their light, lost their life. It would become virtually impossible to find their way out without light.

On our tour it got real dark real fast. The flashlight held by the guide became critically important. To give us a true experience, the guide turned off the lights and we sat in pitch darkness for what seemed like forever. We couldn't even see our hand two inches from our face. Never had I experienced darkness like that. People started to get anxious and the guide finally turned the lights back on. Just in case the lights didn't return, I was secretly trying to retrace my steps in my mind.

Fathers and sons need a strong, clear moral compass. It seems our world is getting more and more confusing and complicated every day. Things that used to be clear are now confusing. Things we used to be certain about are being challenged by our culture or turned totally upside down. This should not surprise us or terrify us. Instead, it should drive us into God's Word for wisdom. His ways never change and His wisdom never waivers.

The Bible describes God's Word as our light. Psalm 119:105 says it this way: "Your word is a lamp to guide my feet and a light for my path." The Word of God provides us with four amazing benefits:

1. **The Word of God is a lamp to our feet.**
   His Word always provides the needed light for decisions and direction today. Every day brings new challenges and choices, and we need to know how to navigate. It helps us walk with confidence right now by revealing stumbling blocks to avoid and making our steps sure. It's impossible to avoid dangerous obstacles in the dark. The lamp also helps us see the hurts and needs of others so we can step in and bring God's light and love to them.

2. **The Word of God is a light to our path.**
   A light also helps us see ahead for decisions about our future. We need God's Word to help us discern our

purpose and pick the path He has chosen for us. His Word helps eliminate anxiety and fear about the future. It gives us wisdom to trust that God has plans for us and that everything is ultimately in His hands. It's impossible to find the right path in utter darkness. As fathers and sons, we need to know God's Word inside and out so we can apply it to our lives. We need to be able to live and lead with confidence and strength instead of with uncertainty and weakness. We need the light of His Word to teach us what is true and right. In 2 Timothy 3:16–17, Paul shares the power of the Word: "All Scripture is inspired by God and is useful to teach us what is true and to make us realize what is wrong in our lives. It corrects us when we are wrong and teaches us to do what is right. God uses it to prepare and equip his people to do every good work."

3. **The Word of God shines light into our character.**
   It reveals what is really going on inside. It shows us what's wrong so we can get it right. It reveals wrong actions and also wrong attitudes. The Word brings a change of heart and a change in behavior. It makes us feel conviction and corrects us when we're not doing the right thing. But it doesn't stop there; it then tells us exactly what to do to get it right. God's Word is necessary for spiritual maturity and godly living.

4. **The Word of God shines light into our circumstances.**
   It helps us see the truth about what we are going through so we can make wise decisions. It helps us see the schemes of the Enemy to deceive, distract, or destroy us so we can take our stand or change course. It's impossible to find our way out of compromising circumstances if

we can't see that we're in them. When we know and read the Word, it gives us skill for living. We learn that Jesus Himself is the Word and the Light of men in John 1:1–5 NIV: "In the beginning was the Word, and the Word was with God, and the Word was God. He was with God in the beginning. Through him all things were made; without him nothing was made that has been made. In him was life, and that life was the light of all mankind. The light shines in the darkness, and the darkness has not overcome it."

There is actually no such thing as darkness. Darkness is just the absence of light, and spiritually speaking, the absence of Jesus. So if you're having a hard time seeing clearly, maybe it's time to turn on the light. Spend time with Jesus. Turn the light on every day and keep the light on. Spend time in His Word daily. One of the greatest things a father can do with his son is to spend time in God's Word together. There is power when you stamp out the darkness together. If you don't, it won't be long before you're stumbling along in darkness. When we turn the light on each day, we discover truth and wisdom. When we lose our light, we lose our life.

TAKE ACTION

1. Read Mark 1:35. What is keeping you from starting each day reading God's Word?

2. Read Psalm 1:1–3 and Hebrews 4:12. What are the benefits of reading and meditating on God's Word?

3. Discuss how you can start the day together turning on the light by spending time in God's Word. Commit to do one thing together and write it here.

Father, thank You for giving us Your Word in the Bible and in the life of Jesus. Give us the strength to read it daily and apply it as a light to all areas of our life. Help us clearly see our path, our character, our circumstances, and our opportunities to be a light for others. Amen.

BEWARE, STRONG ONE

CALLED TO GREATNESS PRINCIPLE
An unguarded strength is a double weakness.

The Bible characters fell on their strengths, never on their weaknesses.
—Oswald Chambers

From a very young age, I have been told that becoming the best means maximizing our strengths and working on our weaknesses. It always seemed like a good strategy. NBA great Michael Jordan said, "My attitude is that if you push me toward something that you think is a weakness, then I will turn that perceived weakness into a strength." Jordon was arguably the best at this. We all, to one degree or another, spend time working to turn weaknesses into strengths.

But how many of us would admit that we turn strengths into weaknesses? Most of us don't even think this is possible. But beware, strong one. If you're not careful, your strengths can quickly become weaknesses without warning.

> Our strengths
> might just be the problem.

When you take a personal strength to the extreme, it's likely to become a weakness. Oftentimes you can't see it; after all, you've been told to focus on your strengths and maximize them. And because you think you're doing the right thing, this unguarded strength causes a blind spot.

For example, my greatest strength is passion; however, when I have too much passion, I become overbearing. I can believe so much in where we need to go and what we need to do, that I crowd out the opinions of others. With my extreme passion, I don't value others' input and wisdom. In my attempt to lead and mobilize others around a great project or idea, I actually end up discouraging the group. My passion, fueled by a will-not-be-denied persistence, can wear people out along the way.

Obviously, that's never my intention. But when our strengths are out of balance or used in excess, they end up having a negative effect. It's troubling to think that the thing you're best at or the very gift that God has blessed you with can become a weakness.

Now I have learned that an unguarded strength is a double weakness. When a friend challenged me with this powerful principle, I quickly thought about several strengths that I had not guarded. Over time, I had become lazy with my strengths and not kept them in check. A strength, gift, or skill can not only lose its impact but also take you down.

If you think you are standing strong, be careful not to fall.
–1 Corinthians 10:12

Moses gives us a great example of how an unguarded strength can become a double weakness. God had a special relationship with Moses; many times Moses actually heard God speak. When He first asked Moses to step up and set the

Israelites free, Moses was timid and lacked confidence in his ability to speak boldly. But over time, Moses saw God use him to do miraculous things and he grew in confidence. So, when God told him to "speak to that rock" to bring water to his people as they wandered in the desert on the way to the Promised Land, Moses made a mistake by relying on himself.

> The LORD said to Moses, "Take the staff, and you and your brother Aaron gather the assembly together. Speak to that rock before their eyes and it will pour out its water. You will bring water out of the rock for the community so they and their livestock can drink." –Numbers 20:7–8 NIV

Moses basically said, "I got this," as he struck the rock twice with his staff instead of obeying and depending on God's power. The entire nation paid the price.

When we are confident in our strengths, we lose dependence on God. We start to believe we don't really need Him, and we try to do everything on our own. We begin trusting in ourselves instead of trusting God to work in us and through us. Even though this works sometimes, we will eventually become dry and empty and reach the end of our capability.

> "Not by might nor by power, but by my Spirit," says the LORD Almighty. –Zechariah 4:6 NIV

There are two keys to making sure a strength remains a strength: *balance* and *blessing.*

First, our strengths must have balance. Every good and perfect gift comes from God. Paul reminds us in 1 Corinthians 12:4 MSG, "God's various gifts are handed out everywhere; but they all originate in God's Spirit." We must find something else that balances it, stabilizes it, and maximizes it. With awareness and accountability, our strengths will be a blessing. Without it, they become a burden. For example, it's dangerous when there is:

- Work without rest
- Passion without humility
- Speaking without listening
- Compassion without truth
- Conviction without forgiveness
- Friendship without accountability
- Discipline without flexibility

Second, we must use our strengths to bless others. The gifts and strengths we've been given are designed to be given away. God pours gifts into us; our job is to pour out what He has poured in. We must use these strengths for the benefit and blessing of others. Use them to bring glory to God at all times. As Paul writes in 1 Corinthians 12:7 MSG, "Each person is given something to do that shows who God is."

Fathers need to help identify and develop their sons' strengths by providing opportunities to utilize and grow in them. Fathers often focus on their sons' weaknesses and become overbearing, negative, and life draining. But when we help our sons identify their unique strengths and gifts, keep them in balance, and use them for the benefit and blessing of others, we help them experience a powerful and meaningful life. Fathers, take the time to validate your sons and let them know how special they are.

So remember: beware, strong one. An unguarded strength is a double weakness. Fathers and sons, know and guard your strengths at all times.

TAKE ACTION

1. Read 1 Corinthians 12:1–11.

2. Share with each other what you think your strengths are. Now ask each other.

3. When used correctly, how do your strengths bless God and others? When out of balance, what do they turn into? What kind of effect do they have on others?

4. How does Satan use your strengths to bring harm and pain when they are used inappropriately?

Lord, I ask that You will use my strengths for Your glory. I ask that each gift, ability, and strength that You have given me becomes a blessing to others, not a curse. I ask You, Lord, to ground each strength You've given me. I pray for wisdom to know that they are Your strengths, not mine. Remove my pride so that my strengths will not be perverted or distorted. Flow through these gifts. Amen.

Never
Too Late

CALLED TO GREATNESS PRINCIPLE
It's never too late to do the right thing.

*He called out to the L*ORD*: "L*ORD *God, please remember me. Strengthen me, God, just once more."*
—Judges 16:28 HCSB

*P*rofessional golfer Blayne Barber had finally qualified for the PGA Tour. It was a dream come true. However, a week after playing in the tournament that qualified him, he couldn't get a leaf out of his mind. Yes, a leaf. In the second round of the tournament, he had accidently brushed a leaf in the bunker on the 13th hole, so he marked his scorecard with a one-shot penalty for the infraction. Later that night, he learned it was a two-shot penalty. He played the final two rounds, but a week later, he didn't have peace signing an incorrect scorecard, so he did the right thing. He disqualified himself, which cost him a spot on the PGA Tour. Blayne lived out the principle, "It's never too late to do the right thing."

When we have to go back and correct something, it's usually hard and involves sacrifice. This is a principle I have to remind myself often, because I am so forward focused and always thinking about what is next. Messing with the past is difficult and complicated. I think to myself, *Why do I need to dig up the past and try to fix things?*

God loves it when we go back, correct it, and make it right. It took integrity and courage for Blayne to go back and disqualify himself, but he will always know that he did the right thing. God was pleased with what Blayne did. Hard but right. Painful but powerful.

My son recently reminded me of how thankful he was that I circled back with him on something I once said to him that needed to be corrected. I'd apologized several days after the incident happened and asked him for forgiveness. Now as an eighteen-year-old, he remembers the conversation five years later. What he remembers is that I was willing to do what it takes to make it right no matter what.

Sometimes it can be hard to do the right thing, but it always results in blessing. There will be a godly harvest when we do the right things for others.

> So let's not get tired of doing what is good. At just the right time we will reap a harvest of blessing if we don't give up. Therefore, whenever we have the opportunity, we should do good to everyone—especially to those in the family of faith. –Galatians 6:9–10

Doing the right thing is always the right thing to do no matter when it is. There is no time limit on doing the right thing. The decisions you make today will be the stories you tell tomorrow, because the stories you're telling today are decisions you made in the past. One day Blayne will be telling his kids about making the right decision even though it was extremely difficult. What type of stories do you want to tell?

If we don't go back and make it right, we will live with guilt and shame; but when we do make it right, we live with freedom and integrity. The choice is yours.

In the Bible, we read about Samson starting out well in life, but he got into a heap of trouble by making some really bad decisions. However, even Samson realized that it wasn't too late to make things right. At the end of his life, he called upon the Lord and did the right thing.

> Then Samson prayed to the LORD, "Sovereign LORD, remember me again. O God, please strengthen me just one more time. With one blow let me pay back the Philistines for the loss of my two eyes." Then Samson put his hands on the two center pillars that held up the temple. Pushing against them with both hands, he prayed, "Let me die with the Philistines." –Judges 16:28–30a

Samson also asked God for strength, which is vital to doing the right thing because many times we are going against the flow. He needed God's power to confront his enemies one last time.

It is easy to do the wrong thing, and it is easy to not try to correct our past mistakes. Many times I find myself going back to my son and asking for forgiveness for the way I responded inappropriately. Sometimes I feel it was a significant thing, but he has completely forgotten about it and it wasn't a big deal. Other times I thought it was a little thing but found out I had wounded his heart. The point is not to determine if it was significant or not; rather, do the right thing and let God work. The Lord will use your obedience and willingness to be open, honest, and vulnerable as you live this principle.

Lord, who can dwell in Your tent?
Who can live on Your holy mountain?
The one who lives honestly,
Practices righteousness,
And acknowledges the truth in his heart.
–Psalm 15:1–2 HCSB

Making things right with others brings closeness with God. Sometimes people don't receive us very well when we try to fix things from the past because they may still have pain and bitterness. But doing the right thing will help others experience God's healing touch by setting them free to experience His forgiveness as well.

There might be friends or family members who are counting on us to go back and make things right. Ask God to help you see things you have done wrong, listen to what He is asking you to do to make it right, and then be obedient and take action out of a spirit of humility. Whether it is days, weeks, months, years, or a lifetime, we need to always do the right thing no matter what the cost. God wants to restore, reconcile, and redeem relationships that have been damaged. Remember, it's never too late to do the right thing.

TAKE ACTION

1. If you were Blayne Barber, would you have gone back and disqualified yourself? Why or why not?

2. What prevents you from going back and doing the right thing?

3. Why is it important to always remember that it's never too late to do the right thing?

4. How can this principle change your father–son relationship?

Father, I know that it is never too late to do the right thing. Give me the understanding to know when I need to go back and do the right thing, and the courage to do it. In Jesus' name, amen.

RUN
YOUR RACE

CALLED TO GREATNESS PRINCIPLE
Keep His pace.

Since we live by the Spirit, let us keep in step with the
Spirit.

–Galatians 5:25 NIV

*A*s I endured another wave of triathletes swimming over the top of me, I was fighting to survive. The words of my friend who is a seasoned triathlete echoed in my mind: "Just run your race." But I had chosen to ignore this most valuable piece of advice, sprinted to the front with the strongest swimmers, and was completely out of gas just two hundred meters into the swim. I had scrapped my pre-race plan to stay to the outside of the pack on the swim, go out easy, and save some energy for the bike and run. I had trained for the three legs of the race, but got derailed right off the bat.

My race plan was good, but I abandoned it. Unfortunately, the emotion of the event got the best of me and I raced ahead of my abilities. The coaching I received was out the window because I thought I could do it on my own. I wanted to win, and was willing to risk it, but I paid a big price for my foolishness.

My kids kept wondering when they would see Dad come out of the water...then they watched for me to come in on the bike... then they watched hundreds of other runners cross the finish line, but I was nowhere in sight. Even though I finished the race, it was a punishing day. I was beaten and exhausted. This was not the way it was supposed to go.

This is true of life as well. When we decide to go ahead of God and do things our own way, we end up beaten and exhausted. And very few will finish the race very strong. That's why so many families are suffering; many dads have abandoned their game plans and are off pursuing their own personal happiness instead of the greatest good: leading their families well. We get derailed by distractions and comparisons and think the grass is greener in somebody else's yard. It's all a lie.

> Distractions look so good at the time,
> but end up so bad in the end.

We get distracted by the things we want to enjoy, but they don't help us get where we want to go. In Hebrews 12:1a, we are told to "strip off every weight that slows us down, especially the sin that so easily trips us up." Sometimes distractions are people and sometimes they are things. Either way, if they are taking your eyes off Jesus, they are a distraction. In verse 2 we are reminded to keep our eyes on Jesus. That focus helps us stay on track.

Comparisons can make us feel better or worse about our own life and make us want to do what others do or have what they have. In the end we stop running our race and join someone else in his or her race. God has a unique path mapped out for each of us. When we try to keep pace with someone else, it usually ends badly. Andy Stanley says "there is no win in comparison." Comparison either makes you feel superior or inferior, and neither one is good for you. And the comparison traps boys and makes them try to be something they're not.

Jesus gives us simple instructions for how to keep His pace. In Matthew 11:29–30, He tells us to take His yoke upon us:

> Take my yoke upon you. Let me teach you, because I am humble and gentle at heart, and you will find rest for your souls. For my yoke is easy to bear, and the burden I give you is light.

The image here is one of putting the yoke of an ox over your shoulders and being paired with Jesus. In order for this team to work properly and plow the field, you have to be in step with each other. Otherwise, you will be pushing and pulling each other and the field will be a mess. When we listen to His voice and learn from Him, we live at a pace that is pleasing to Him.

> Fathers and sons need to be in sync with each other.

We both need to put on the yoke of Christ and make it our goal to walk closely with Him. When we both walk closely with Jesus, we generally start to see eye-to-eye on a lot more things. And, we begin to trust that each one of us is tuning his ear to listen to God's voice. We grow in confidence of the key decisions that are made.

If we want to finish the race, we have to keep His pace. When we do, we can be assured of His presence and His purpose. When we abandon the plan and pursue our own purpose is when we get into trouble.

> Be patient, think long-term,
> and do it the right way.

This was God's instruction for His people, because He knew best. He was telling them, "Run your race. Keep My pace. Stay in step with the Holy Spirit. Don't go out too fast and run out of gas. My pace is the best pace. Trust Me, I know what I am doing." Staying in step with God means that you follow in His footsteps. You don't go where He doesn't lead.

Run your race. Keep His pace. Stay in step with the Holy Spirit. Let Him lead you and teach you the race pace that works for you. In the end, you can trust His plan, enjoy His promises, and finish your race well.

TAKE ACTION

1. How would you describe the pace of your life right now? Easy, just right, or too fast?

2. In what ways have you abandoned the plan and gone out in your own strength?

3. What are the benefits of running your race at the pace God has set for you?

4. What things need to change so you can keep His pace and keep in step with the Spirit?

Father, help us to be a father and son who listen for Your voice together. Help us to stay in step with Your Spirit and stay on the road that leads to life. Show us how to follow in Your footsteps, run our race, and keep Your pace. Amen.

MENTOR ME

Mentors take you to the next level.

Leadership is getting someone to do what they don't want to do, to achieve what they want to achieve.

–Tom Landry

Every year, CrossFit crowns one man and one woman with the title of "Fittest Man on Earth" and "Fittest Woman on Earth." The CrossFit Games, comprised of the top fifty men and the top fifty women from around the globe, are the world's premier test to find the fittest on earth. For the past four years, the Fittest Man on Earth title has belonged to Rich Froning, a sold-out Christian with Galatians 6:14 boldly tattooed on his side.

CrossFit has inspired millions to test their personal limits and train in ways most thought impossible, regardless of age. My friend Dr. Landan Webster, a former college athlete and now a doctor of chiropractic, is one of those guys. He used his built-in competitiveness and trained alongside some incredibly fit athletes who pushed each other to be their best. But, in his own words, "I never had a mentor. I never gave anyone permission to truly coach me, evaluate me, or help me get to the next level."

As iron sharpens iron, so one person sharpens another.
–Proverbs 27:17 NIV

But everything changed when Webster chose mentors and gave them permission to push him. He asked them to show and tell, critique everything, and fully engage. The mentors did everything they could to get everything out of him. He needed their knowledge, motivation, encouragement, and belief to get it out. In the end, he achieved incredible goals that never would have been possible otherwise.

> Dads are designed by God to be
> the best mentors for their sons.

God builds in a bond of love between father and son that goes all the way back to His own relationship with His Son, Jesus. Love and affection between father and son are in His perfect design. The father's pleasure rests on his son.

God has purposefully placed dads with their boys to show and tell. We are designed to do life together in perhaps the closest relationship in life next to marriage. Over the years, I've had my boys by my side for virtually everything, teaching them and showing them key things in life—building, fixing, relating, playing, overcoming, celebrating, competing, recovering, serving, giving, loving, you name it. Sometimes I got it right and other times I didn't, but they've learned from all those situations.

Follow my example as I follow the example of Christ.
–1 Corinthians 11:1 NIV

In this passage, Paul defines mentoring in the simplest terms. He was the ultimate mentor. He lived his life in plain view for all to see and taught and encouraged others to imitate him. He shared his strengths and weaknesses, his victories and struggles. Dads don't have to be perfect because mentoring is about sharing mistakes more than successes. When sons give fathers permission to guide and direct, they will grow in all aspects of life.

There are four significant benefits when fathers mentor their sons:

1. **Great dads are intentional about mentoring, and their sons get better sooner.**
   The best dads realize they are willing to walk with their sons in the journey of life. They do more showing than they do telling. Trust is learned and confidence is earned through showing. When sons put what their fathers show and tell into practice, they get results and begin to believe.

2. **Great dads know their son's current condition and can see their future capabilities.**
   Sons are not limited by their father's thoughts or feelings, but instead driven by their belief in their fathers. Most of our limits originate in our minds. Mentors know how to speak encouraging words of life. They understand that words have the power of life and death; they also have directional impact on our lives like a rudder on a ship. Dads are designed to see ahead through God's eyes and help their sons find their purpose and path.

3. **Great dads believe in their sons more than their sons believe in themselves.**
   Dads always believe the best in their boys. Always. This never waivers. They know how to take their sons to the

next level and prepare them for challenges and circumstances, as well as how to push them beyond their limits and prepare them to overcome. Dads are more concerned with the condition of their heart and breathing life into their son's soul with encouragement, words of affirmation, and unconditional love.

4. **Great dads make the most of every moment because they separate fact from fiction.**
    Dads pass on truth that has been proven. They don't have time for guesswork, and neither do their sons. It's more about showing and less about telling. And dads learn how to use victories and defeats to develop character. Failure is just an opportunity to learn and grow.

But perhaps the greatest discovery I've made is the principle I call "mentor up." This year, my second son got serious about weight lifting for his sport, and we regularly went to the gym together. I got to witness his energy, intensity, and drive up close—and the approach he modeled made me push harder and get better results than I had in years. He was mentoring me by example.

> Don't let anyone think less of you because you are young. Be an example to all believers in what you say, in the way you live, in your love, your faith, and your purity. –1 Timothy 4:12

He has, along with his brothers, modeled other qualities like focus, discipline, overcoming adversity, perseverance, courage, and the importance of not taking yourself too seriously. Sons have a unique opportunity, right now, to be an example for their dads. God is calling sons to be mentored and to mentor up.

Dads and their sons must do life together if they want to be their best for God. We will not instinctively get stronger, work harder, seek more, or grow unless we have a mentor to show and tell. Dads, lead, guide, and push your sons to be their best. Sons, live in such a way that you inspire your dad. Help each other become who God made you to be—and take your life to the next level.

TAKE ACTION

1. Read Philippians 3:17. Why is it important to be mentored and follow the Christ-like example of others? In what ways can dads help their sons be their best?

2. What barriers or limits do you have that might be keeping you from God's best? How might your dad/son help you achieve breakthrough?

3. Review 1 Timothy 4:12. Talk about ways that sons can mentor up by example.

4. Dads, write two names of people you can ask to mentor you. Invite them this week.

Father, thank You for establishing a built-in bond between fathers and sons. Thank You that in Your perfect design You will use an imperfect father to raise up the next generation of men. Thank You that sons are called to mentor up as well. Bring us together in everyday circumstances for show and tell. Use our relationship to make us our best. Amen.

26

The New Four-Letter Word

CALLED TO GREATNESS PRINCIPLE
Finish what you start.

Consider it a great joy, my brothers, whenever you experience various trials, knowing that the testing of your faith produces endurance. But endurance must do its complete work, so that you may be mature and complete, lacking nothing.

–James 1:2–4 HCSB

*S*everal years ago, the football team at the Oscoda Area High School in Michigan cancelled the last five games of the season as a result of going 0–4 and having not scored a point. I know going winless and scoreless has a sting to it, but my heart hurts thinking that someone gave up on a group of athletes. I think about the possible victories those athletes will never experience. I don't mean on-the-field victories. Yes, they probably would have finished 0–9, but it's not about the scoreboard or the win–loss column.

It's about the life victories that they will not experience this season. I guess they had never heard the famous Winston Churchill quote, "Never give in—never, never, never, never, in nothing great or small, large or petty, never give in..."

The new four-letter word is QUIT.

Quit is something that has permeated our society and regretfully become a core value that people live by. People quit without giving it another thought. However, I believe the word needs to be removed from our vocabulary. Not only is it a curse word, but it's also a curse to all who live by it.

I can hear, twenty years from now, those athletes saying that that they wish the coaches had not given up on them. Those athletes will remember that season their entire life. Even if they continued the season and went winless and scoreless, it could have been a defining moment that could have developed character in them. It's in the struggle and strain that God shapes us and molds us.

It's in defeat that we learn the most, not in quitting.

I will never forget the conversation I had with a sixteen-year-old boy during a weekend retreat; it burdened my heart greatly. During free time, I saw him sitting by himself with his head in his hands. Obviously something was troubling him, so I sat down next to him to help. Noticing that he was crying, I simply asked what was wrong. Having had the opportunity to work in youth ministry for years, I was prepared for the typical response dealing with the usual issues: girlfriend problems, alcohol or drugs, friendship struggles, or school issues. I was shocked when he said, "I hate that my parents let me quit everything I start." He went on to explain that everything he started, he quit. He then said, "I just wish they would make me finish what I started." Wow. Usually I hear the exact opposite: "I hate that my parents make me finish everything I start."

I realized that day more than ever that young people need support, direction, and encouragement to finish strong. He recognized that he was weak and that his tendency would be to quit when things got tough, but he wished his parents would help him to finish well. This conversation has helped shape me as a parent. We have incorporated a family rule: *What you start, you finish.* Often we will say, "Brittons don't quit!" It's an easy way to reinforce the value of finishing everything we start.

With my son, whatever he starts, he is encouraged to finish. If he realizes that he doesn't want to continue because of various reasons, he knows he can discuss stopping after it is over. Stopping afterward is different from quitting during. When he was in eighth grade, he wanted to quit lacrosse. We are a lacrosse family, with all the kids playing and my wife and I coaching. He was feeling the pressure to perform and didn't want to keep playing. As we talked through it after the season, he realized that most of the pressure was self-imposed. He decided to persevere, and he is now one of the team leaders on his varsity high school team.

> So be truly glad. There is wonderful joy ahead, even though you must endure many trials for a little while. These trials will show that your faith is genuine. It is being tested as fire tests and purifies gold—though your faith is far more precious than mere gold. So when your faith remains strong through many trials, it will bring you much praise and glory and honor on the day when Jesus Christ is revealed to the whole world. —1 Peter 1:6–7

We believe that God will honor and bless the faithfulness of His children. Our families should be a place of fertile ground to cultivate a spirit of finishing. The four-letter word *quit* should be removed from our conversations. Paul reminds us in Galatians 6:9 the reward of not quitting: "So let's not get tired of doing what is good. At just the right time we will reap a harvest of blessing if we don't give up."

Christ did not quit on the cross. Paul did not give up preaching the gospel when he was thrown into jail. Daniel did not stop praying when he was thrown into the lions' den. It is easy to give up when it gets tough. However, when it gets tough and we press on, God is glorified. Our goal is to keep our eyes fixed on Jesus so that we finish strong.

TAKE ACTION

1. When do you feel like quitting?

2. When was the last time you stuck it out even though you wanted to quit? What did you learn from that experience?

3. Who in the Bible quit? Who persevered?

4. What are ways you make sure that you finish strong?

5. How can you encourage each other not to quit?

Father, help me when things get tough. I feel at times like I am going under and I want to quit. Show me the blessing that is waiting for me. It is hard to be faithful in times of pain and struggle. Fill me with Your Holy Spirit, so others will see You in times of trouble. Thank You for the strain, Lord.

27

STAND STRONG

Be unshakable!

It's not hard to make decisions when you know what your values are.

–Roy E. Disney

Every father wants to pass on a set of core values to his son. Core values really become the essence of who we are; they capture what we believe, how we think, and how we act. They are, simply put, the stuff we're made of. They're the heart values that mold and shape us. Our values define what's most important to us and guide us as we embark on our mission. Core values help us navigate the challenges of life and stay true north. What we value most, we protect. Early on, values can be something we strive to live up to. Later on, they define what we stand for.

The US Marine Corps has three core values: *honor, courage,* and *commitment. Honor* forms the bedrock of their character and holds them to the highest standard and an uncompromising code of ethical and moral behavior. *Courage* is the mental, moral, and physical strength to take the right action under great stress and pressure, and even in the face of fear. *Commitment* is the spirit of dedication, determination, and discipline needed in their relentless pursuit of excellence.

Sign me up. Those values inspire me. Now I might add *faith* and *love* to the mix, but you could build a life on these. Our buddy Jon Gordon said, "If you want to build up, you have to first dig deep and develop your foundation. Build the foundation with values, principles, and habits that will help you soar."

You build a man the same way you build a cathedral, from the ground up. In order for a man to stand, he has to have a solid foundation of faith in Christ. Jesus is the embodiment of these characteristics and more. When we build our lives on Jesus and His Word, when we put His Word into practice, we are able to stand in the midst of everything life throws at us (Matthew 7:24–27).

As fathers pass on their core values to their sons, it's with the purpose of preparing them for life. Too many men have a shaky spiritual foundation or no foundation at all. This leads them to compromise, take shortcuts, and make excuses for why things didn't turn out quite like they envisioned.

The most common compromises are in the areas of lying, cheating, alcohol, drugs, and sexual immorality. When we lower the bar of expectations for our sons, we set them up for failure. When we lower the bar for ourselves, we lose our right to lead.

Daniel and his friends (Shadrach, Meshach, and Abednego) serve as great role models for how to stand strong under incredible pressure.

- In Daniel 1, they refused to violate their conscience by eating food from the king's table because it had been offered to idols. They chose God's ways and were rewarded with incredible health and favor.

- In Daniel 3, they refused to bow and worship false gods even under the threat of certain death in the blazing furnace. God protected them and delivered them from the fire.
- In Daniel 6, Daniel refused to stop his devotion to God in prayer and was thrown into the lions' den. God shut the mouths of the lions and rescued Daniel.

These four young men showed us how to stand strong for God on a solid foundation. They were unshakable. And here's why: They knew God personally, they knew themselves, they knew their values, and they were ready for adversity.

Fathers need to train their sons how to stand strong in this culture:

1. **Anticipate**
   I believe in advanced decision making—anticipating situations I may face and knowing what I will do before it happens; that way I am rarely surprised or caught flat-footed and unprepared. I believe Daniel and the other three knew opposition was coming, anticipated situations they might face, and made decisions in advance about what they would do if they faced it. They were prepared to stand strong.

2. **Ask**
   I have always told my boys to ask a simple question when deciding what to do: *Is it wise?* In other words, will this decision move me toward God's best for my life? Based on who I am, the person I want to be, and the dreams

God has placed in my heart, is this wise? Will my decision ultimately result in God's glory?

3. **Act**

I believe decisive action is a demonstration of internal conviction. Courage isn't the absence of fear; it's taking action in the face of fear. Daniel and his friends were ready to stand for what they believed from day one. They had formed spiritual habits that led to a strong spiritual foundation. They had dug deep with God, and their faith was an everyday, every-minute interaction. It was Daniel's habit to pray three times each day. The others had formed a single-hearted devotion to God and had unshakable confidence in His capabilities. They were ready to act. Sometimes you will advance into battle and other times you will avoid compromising situations.

As men, we must be prepared to stand strong. We need to be willing to:

- **stand against** the evil that threatens our hearts and homes;
- **stand with** those who are defenseless—the least, the last, and the lost; and
- **stand for** the love, compassion, and grace of Jesus.

In a culture that will challenge everything we stand for, fathers and sons need to stand together and stand strong. Build a strong foundation on your faith in Jesus. Establish habits that deepen that foundation around your core values, and get ready to make a difference. Anticipate, ask, and act. Be unshakable!

TAKE ACTION

1. Read Ephesians 6:10–18. How does this passage help you get ready for the battle? Discuss each piece of the armor and how you can put it on in a practical sense.

2. Make a list of core values that you live by together as a father and son. Talk them through and try to agree on three or four. Write these down and find a Bible verse for each.

3. Talk through the three steps of standing strong: *anticipate*, *ask*, and *act*. Put common situations you may face through the process and make decisions in advance.

Father, thank You for the examples in the Bible of great men who were able to stand strong under great pressure. Help us to establish our foundation of core values, anticipate situations we may face, and make decisions in advance. Help us be unshakable. Amen.

28

IT'S ALL GONNA MELT SOMEDAY

CALLED TO GREATNESS PRINCIPLE
Hold light and live free.

My home is in Heaven. I'm just traveling through this world.

–Billy Graham

eing a teenager in the '80s, I was blessed with the arrival of Christian punk bands—a blessing for me, but a burden for my parents. One of my favorite bands was One Bad Pig, who had songs like, "Smash the Guitar," "Cut Your Hair," and my all-time favorite, "Ice Cream Sundae." They were described as "quite possibly the most popular hard-punk act to arise within the Christian music scene." The one line I loved most from their song "Ice Cream Sundae" was:

"The world is like an ice cream sundae. It's all gonna melt someday."

As followers of Christ, we know that what we see will not last. All the stuff of the world will melt one day, but we live as if it is eternal. What we can see is temporary, but what we can't see is eternal. Paul reminds us of this truth:

So we do not focus on what is seen, but on what is unseen;
for what is seen is temporary, but what is unseen is eternal.
–2 Corinthians 4:18 NIV

It may sound a little crazy to focus on the unseen. If we can't
see it, then why is Paul encouraging us in 1 Corinthians 4:18 to
focus on it? The world is the *seen*, and heaven is the *unseen*. He
knows that nothing here lasts. We spend so much time, energy,
and attention on the here and now. Yet compared to eternity,
it's like a couple of seconds. Paul is warning us about the brevity
of life and the insignificance of things on earth.

Can you imagine staying in a hotel for a night and replac-
ing the room's contents with your own furniture and pictures?
Setting it up like it was your home? Maybe you could even get
a really nice big-screen television for better viewing. People
would consider you nuts to go to that extreme for one night or
even a week. I'm sure the Lord looks at us in the same way. He
might say to us, "Hey, why are you are so consumed with your
few seconds on earth? You are spending an incredible amount
of time and money on the very things that will not last. It's all
gonna melt someday."

> Life is a vapor.

If your focus is on the seen, you will hold onto things tightly
and live a hard life. If your focus is on the unseen, you will hold
onto things lightly and live free. The tighter we hold to the
earth, the more we quench life. Life is really short; it's a mist.

Come now, you who say, "Today or tomorrow we will
travel to such and such a city and spend a year there and
do business and make a profit." You don't even know what
tomorrow will bring—what your life will be! For you are like

smoke that appears for a little while, then vanishes. –James
4:13–14 HCSB

Holding this world loosely is a concept that hit home for me
several days before my father passed away from his battle with
leukemia, when I noticed a book on heaven next to his bed.
One of his good friends had dropped it off to encourage him.
I asked him if he'd read it, and he smiled and said, "Why do I
need to read about it when I will be experiencing it shortly?"
His perspective changed when he knew he was coming close to
the end. The things that were important in his life, like people
and the things of God, became the most important things. His
walk with the Lord became sweeter each day. He realized his
life was a bit of smoke that was vanishing quickly. My dad was
holding this world loosely, and he was free. There was peace,
because death did not have a hold on his life, nor did this earth.

> Only one life, twill soon be past,
> only what's done for Christ will last. –C. T. Studd

Each one of us must live with an eternal perspective. We are
called to do good works that God has prepared in advance for
us to do. We are all called to build on the foundation of Christ.
And all of our work will be tested to see if it's temporary or
eternal.

Anyone who builds on that foundation may use a variety of
materials—gold, silver, jewels, wood, hay, or straw. But on
the judgment day, fire will reveal what kind of work each
builder has done. The fire will show if a person's work has
any value. If the work survives, that builder will receive a
reward. But if the work is burned up, the builder will suffer

great loss. The builder will be saved, but like someone barely escaping through a wall of flames. —1 Corinthians 3:12–15

Swallow a healthy dose of heaven daily. God desires for you to set your mind on things above so that you can live free now. Don't get trapped by this world. Most of us are all weighed down by the temporary stuff. The funny thing is that we never see materialism in the mirror, but it's easy to spot it everywhere around us. If we're honest, we're holding way too tightly to the things that don't count and not investing in the things that will live on.

People who hold this world lightly stick out. Their life is marked with peace. They find the time to care about the important things and don't sweat the small stuff. Their filter is "heaven is my home, not this earth." Focus on heaven and live free today.

Fathers and sons, it's all gonna melt one day. Be resolved to focus on the unseen, not the seen. Ask the Lord to help remove the things that blur your vision. When we focus on the world, we hold tightly. But if we focus on heaven, we hold lightly.

TAKE ACTION

1. What have you won or accomplished in the past that was significant at the time but now isn't a big deal? What changed?

2. Why is it so easy to focus on the seen (the world), and why is it so hard to focus on the unseen (heaven)?

3. List three ways that can help you keep your focus on the unseen. Share with each other your three ways.

4. Extra verses to study: Philippians 3:20–21, Revelation 21:4.

Lord Jesus, I am confessing that it is hard not to focus on and pursue the things of this world. Empty me of the desires of the world and instead help me crave the things that are unseen—the eternal things. I ask for a godly perspective as I serve You. My life is only a vapor and I want every moment to count. I know that it is all going to melt someday, so help me to live that way. In Jesus' name, amen.

29

Go
All-Out

CALLED TO GREATNESS PRINCIPLE
Make it count.

Count your days and make your days count.
—Andy Stanley

My friend Karen Dub's job is to train the best in the world to be even better. As a master trainer, she trains Olympic athletes to compete on the world's greatest athletic stage. Her goal is to see top athletes maximize their gifts and opportunities so they will experience the thrill of victory and not the agony of defeat. She wants every Olympic competitor to make his or her performance count.

> Go all-out to make it count.

One of the athletes she trained is a pentathlon athlete named Suzanne Stettinius, who made Team USA for the 2012 Olympics. Within days of making the team, she relocated to the Olympic Training Center (OTC) in Colorado Springs, Colorado. At the OTC, every aspect of the athletes' lives are mapped out. The OTC controls the food they eat, the sleep they get, the training they do, and, believe it or not, even the thoughts they think. As Suzanne first entered the world-class weight room, she saw a quote hanging above the door: *Enter these doors with an unrelenting sense of urgency.* The best athletes in the world seem to understand the need to go all-out to make it count.

My boys have, from their earliest days, had a desire to do something great with their lives. I don't know if it came from watching super-hero movies and cartoons or from fighting epic airsoft battles in the backyard. Whatever it is, it's real. They want opportunities to do great things—to be a hero. And I have done my best to keep those dreams alive. They want their life to count and to make the most of their opportunities.

Jesus illustrates this innate desire and make-it-count principle in the parable of the money:

> [A man going on a long trip] called together his servants and entrusted his money to them while he was gone. He gave five bags of silver to one, two bags of silver to another, and one bag of silver to the last—dividing it in proportion to their abilities. He then left on his trip. The servant who received the five bags of silver began to invest the money and earned five more. The servant with two bags of silver also went to work and earned two more. But the servant who received the one bag of silver dug a hole in the ground and hid the master's money. –Matthew 25:14–18

The first two servants made the most of their opportunity. They immediately took responsibility to multiply what they had been trusted with. They saw the opportunity and diligently went to work while the third servant buried the money in fear. Maybe he was afraid he would lose it. In the end, all he had was excuses. He was not willing to go all-out. Great men realize they have to reject fear, distractions, shortcuts, and excuses;

they must maintain laser-like focus to go all-out to make their lives count.

It's not a matter of where you start, but where you finish.

The question is never *how much do I have?* The question is always *what will I do with it?* It's not a matter of how much you have, but what you do with what you have. The size of the gift, potential, or opportunity doesn't matter. The servant who started with five bags and the other who started with two got the same response from the man when he returned from his trip. The man was full of praise, saying:

> Well done, my good and faithful servant. You have been faithful in handling this small amount, so now I will give you many more responsibilities. Let's celebrate together!
> –Matthew 25:23

We all have gifts and opportunities to make a difference for others. Maybe it's with school. Maybe it's with a particular talent we have. Maybe it's with our friendships. Oftentimes, we make it count the most by doing the little things behind the scenes. It's in the small acts of kindness and words of encouragement. It's in the everyday generosity when we give to those who have need. It's in serving those who need a helping hand. It's in sacrificing our own desires and putting others before ourselves.

With great opportunity comes great responsibility.

In Luke 12:48, we are reminded that from those who are given much, much is required. When we are blessed with a lot, we must be even more responsible with what we do with it. We are not blessed just for us, but for others. There are people who are counting on us.

So be careful how you live. Don't live like fools, but like those who are wise. Make the most of every opportunity in these evil days. —Ephesians 5:15

In order for fathers and sons to make it count, they will need to know what to say no to as much as what to say yes to. Some things need to go—some distractions or interruptions, some bad friendships, you name it—so we can do the best on those things we say yes to.

I've heard it said, "If tomorrow wasn't promised, what would you do with today?" Remember that life is short, and approach each day and every opportunity with an unrelenting sense of urgency to make a difference. Whether you have a lot or a little, do a lot with it. See opportunities and seize the day. Go all-out and make it count.

TAKE ACTION

1. Are you living with a sense of urgency to make your life count, or are you going through the motions?

2. What are the most important gifts or opportunities you have been given? List them here. Are you maximizing them? Share them with each other.

3. What good things might you have to say no to so you can say yes to the things that matter most? What one thing will you do today to make your day count?

Father, thank You for giving us this one life to live. Help us to take whatever You've given us and make it count. Help us to do the little unseen things that serve others. Help us to live in such a way that we honor You and make a difference for eternity. Help us to go all-out to make it count. Amen.

30

My
Top 10

CALLED TO GREATNESS PRINCIPLE
Cultivate a life of gratitude.

As we express our gratitude, we must never forget that the highest appreciation is not to utter words, but to live by them.

–John F. Kennedy

 love ESPN's Top 10 Plays of the Day. There is something about a few minutes of sports highlights that makes me want to lace up the shoes and put on the jersey again. Even though ESPN's Top 10 list is my favorite, there are many others out there. Certainly, David Letterman made it famous with his comical late-night list, but did you know that God created the original Top 10 list a long time ago? It's called the Ten Commandments.

At the end of each year, I see lots of Top 10 lists recapping various things from the past year. This prompted me to start my own list, but it's not like the others. I call it my "Top 10 to Thank This Year" list. My list focuses on meaningful relationships that have made a significant impact on my life. I have exactly 365 days during the year to improve, grow, learn, and get stretched. As I consider what changes have taken place in my life, I realize I haven't done it on my own. It takes a host of other people investing in and influencing me along the way.

My list contains friends, co-workers, and some people whom I've never met. At the end of the year, I go back and remember the people who invested in me. Realizing that it is the power of others that makes the most significant difference in my life, I want to let them know how they have touched me. These are the people who have poured out the things that God has poured into them. They've encouraged, educated, and inspired me to grow in my walk with Christ and become more than I imagined.

As Howard Hendricks reminds us, impact always happens up close. It's easy to impress but hard to impact. Impacting takes time, effort, and intentionality. Having people who are willing to take the time to invest in me is honoring and humbling. I've been shaped and developed by so many, and I want to make sure they know that I appreciate them.

> I always thank God for you because of his grace given you in Christ Jesus. –1 Corinthians 1:4 NIV

What a blessing for them and for me when I tell them how they changed my life. This is not the typical call or e-mail. Unfortunately, it's rare to take the time to think about those who have made a mark on our lives. It's even rarer to take the time and effort to go back and let them know. We all have a great opportunity to encourage others by personally communicating our gratitude.

In Luke 17:15–18, we have an example of the one leper out of ten who went back and thanked Jesus. This one leper started the 10 Percent Club—the few who are willing to express their gratitude. It has been said that unexpressed gratitude is ingratitude. My Top 10 is an annual discipline that helps me be part of the 10 Percent Club.

> One of them, when he saw that he was healed, came back to Jesus, shouting, "Praise God!" He fell to the ground at Jesus' feet, thanking him for what he had done. This man was a Samaritan. Jesus asked, "Didn't I heal ten men? Where are the other nine? Has no one returned to give glory to God except this foreigner?"

Jesus was clearly disappointed that only one returned to express gratitude, not because he needed it but because the other nine had denied giving glory to God for what He had done. It's almost like they had taken this miracle for granted. They wanted to be healed but didn't have time to thank the Healer. They lacked a thankful heart.

Cultivating an attitude of gratitude as a lifestyle is a vital part of our family; I believe that the family is the most important place to model it. Busyness, entitlement, and selfishness are the enemies of gratitude. Teaching my son to never miss an opportunity and to go back like the one leper did and express thanks demonstrates what a real man of God does. Many times people have told me that my son went out of his way to thank them. Mission accomplished.

Developing a posture of gratitude on a daily basis helps it become a habit in our lives; it becomes part of who we are and how we do life every day. It's not a once-a-year exercise. It turns out that expressing gratitude also has incredible physical, emotional, and relational benefits as well. It's impossible to be stressed and thankful at the same time. And gratitude is like a muscle: the more we exercise it, the stronger it grows in our life.

Through this process, I'm also able to evaluate my own life and ask myself if I have lived in such a way as to make the Top 10 list of others. Would I be on my son's list? Have I been intentional about investing in others in a significant way? Was I doing everything I could to be a blessing to them?

> Let me say first that I thank my God through Jesus Christ for all of you, because your faith in him is being talked about all over the world. –Romanss 1:8

As fathers and sons, we understand that each of us has great capacity to impact and influence others by expressing gratitude. You never know just how much someone might need to hear from you; their bucket might be empty, and a thankful word might restore purpose and passion when they need it most. It's time to aim for being a Top 10 in someone's life. God placed us here to make a difference in the lives of others, just as they make a difference for us. So what are you waiting for? Go and be used by God to be a difference maker, and thank those who have invested in you.

TAKE ACTION

1. **Create space:** Spend some time praying and thinking about who has impacted your life the most and how. Think through all your relationships.

2. **Grab a pen:** Write out a Top 10 list of your own, but don't worry about ranking people.

3. **Shout-out:** Bless the people you listed and give them a shout-out. Call or e-mail them and let them know that they made the list and why.

4. **Share:** Discuss your list with each other. Give a brief reason why each person is on your list.

Father, thank You for placing others in my path to bless, encourage, and guide me. Show me who has impacted my life and how. I pray that You would use me to do the same for others. In Jesus' name I pray, amen.

31

THE POWER OF MOMENTUM

CALLED TO GREATNESS PRINCIPLE
Keep moving toward God's best.

The world is wide, and I will not waste my life in friction when it could be turned into momentum.

–Frances E. Willard

Several years ago, my boys and I decided to enter the Grand Prix Pinewood Derby car races at our church. We got the car kits, pulled out all the materials to make the car, and set up a workshop in the garage. I read the directions carefully and made sure we met all the criteria for design, size, and weight. The cars were beautiful, and we were certain we would win.

Race day came and we presented our cars for initial inspection. They met the requirements, but after holding some of the other kids' cars, I knew we were in trouble; their cars were noticeably heavier and ours came in well under the maximum weight allowed. I remained optimistic, but as the boys carefully placed their cars on the track—heat after heat—not one of our cars crossed the finish line. They simply did not have enough momentum to maintain their speed and finish the race.

> Positive momentum gives us
> a sense of possibility, optimism, and success.

We can easily see the power of momentum at work in sports, but it's also alive and well in everyday life. We define life momentum as "movement toward or away from God's best." We have experienced this force at work in all aspects of life—physically, mentally, emotionally, spiritually, relationally, and financially—for better or worse. Momentum can be positive or negative. It's also highly contagious to others. It's important that fathers and sons are able to see this force at work and harness it to be their best for God and others.

Positive momentum feels good because we have purpose, passion, and power. It gives us energy too. Everything seems to be in sync. If I have positive momentum with my physical health, I'm probably making good choices with my foods and feeling energized and strong. The greater the positive momentum, the easier it is to overcome challenges and obstacles. It makes big things seem small. Positive momentum is movement toward God's best.

> Negative momentum makes us feel helpless,
> hopeless, and worthless.

Nothing seems to be going right. Sometimes we can just be plain stuck. If I have negative momentum with my finances, I'm probably spending more than I have and can't get out of debt. The greater the negative momentum, the harder it is to overcome challenges. It makes small things seem big. You've heard the expression "the straw that broke the camel's back," right? Negative momentum takes us away from God's best.

But the good news is this: we can actually change the momentum we are experiencing if we want to. The choices we make have a direct effect on the momentum we experience. Momentum is largely determined by this simple equation:

$$\text{Momentum} = (\text{Attitudes} + \text{Actions})^X$$

We are fully in control of our attitudes and actions. A negative attitude never makes a positive improvement. And intentions never change anything without action. But the real power of momentum is found in the X-factor. What power will we rely on? Will we surrender control to the Holy Spirit or will we continue to rely on our own limited strength?

> The Spirit of God, who raised Jesus from the dead, lives in you. –Roman 8:11

The Spirit of God gives us unstoppable power to overcome any challenge. We are never helpless or hopeless as long as we have God's presence and power. Moses wouldn't make a move without God. Gideon confirmed God's instruction before stepping out. We can do nothing apart from Jesus.

Momentum is demonstrated clearly in this short passage in Hebrews:

> Such a large crowd of witnesses is all around us! So we must get rid of everything that slows us down, especially the sin that just won't let go. And we must be determined to run the race that is ahead of us. We must keep our eyes on Jesus, who leads us and makes our faith complete. –Hebrews 12:1–2

Here are the four F's of positive momentum that will get us moving toward God's best:

1. **Faith**
   Expect God's best for His glory and our ultimate good. Throughout the Bible we see stories of how God turns

the impossible into the possible. God can do more than we can ever ask or imagine (Ephesians 3:20). Faith finds opportunities with every obstacle. Faith believes in spite of circumstances or challenges. Faith often requires that we step out before we find out. Put your faith in action. Jesus states it clearly in Luke 18:27 NIV: "What is impossible with man is possible with God."

2. **Focus**

Where focus goes, energy flows. Our first focus must always be to keep our eyes on Jesus. We have to get our eyes off the challenge and focus on God's capability. Focus on what you can do instead of what you can't and do something differently. Focus drives faith and action. Hebrews 12:2 ERV is a key passage on focus: "We must never stop looking to Jesus. He is the leader of our faith, and he is the one who makes our faith complete."

3. **Freedom**

Forget the past and focus on the prize. We have to throw off the stuff that is holding us back and weighing us down. Focus on how far you've come instead of how far you have to go. Be fearless. Don't be afraid to make mistakes; it's all part of the process. Go make a play. Paul reminds us in Philippines 3:13–14 about forgetting the past: "I focus on this one thing: Forgetting the past and looking forward to what lies ahead, I press on to reach the end of the race and receive the heavenly prize."

4. **Fans**

We need a small group of trusted friends who are committed to helping us be our very best in Christ. When things look the worst, they give their best. When you're out of energy, they fill your tank. When you're down, they lift you up. That small group of faith-filled friends keeps us moving toward God's best.

Fathers and sons can literally change the momentum of their home, their community, and their life. We need to be on the lookout for momentum and take action to change it or create it. Relying on the X-factor, the power of God at work in us and through us, makes all the difference in the world. Momentum is created and sustained through a positive attitude and consistent action under God's power. Small choices lead to big changes. The right actions done with the right attitude consistently over time will result in positive momentum. Keep moving toward God's best.

TAKE ACTION

1. As you look at each area of your life, do you have positive or negative momentum? Talk about each area together.

2. Discuss ways to invite God in to help reverse the negative and turn it around.

3. What is one thing you can do that will have the greatest positive impact—on your spiritual life, relationships, thoughts, etc.?

Father, we desire to have positive momentum—to be moving toward Your best in every area of our lives. Thank You that even in challenging times, how we respond can keep us moving toward Your best. Help us to recognize it when we are stuck or negative so we can turn it around. Amen.

More from Dan & Jimmy

WisdomWalks is a real-life guide for walking purposefully with God and living the life of significance you were created for. Forty intentional, spiritual, life-changing connections will transform the way you think and do life. Each WisdomWalk features one key life principle, a real-life story, questions for individuals or groups, action steps, and lots more—all based on the truths and wisdom of God's Word. **Perfect for parents, coaches, and leaders to pass the torch to the next generation.**

"A spiritual home run for personal growth, discipleship, and mentoring. Biblical, practical, inspiring, and digestible! I'm all in!" —**Chip Ingram,** Living on the Edge

"I know these two FCA leaders personally, and you will be blessed by their powerful insights!" —**James B. "Buck" McCabe,** CFO, Chick-fil-A, Inc.

True Competitor is an experience so powerful it will transform your life on and off the field and impact teammates, coaches, and generations to come. Want an unstoppable faith that packs a punch in the gym, in the locker room, at home, and in all your relationships? *True Competitor* will ignite your passion to live intentionally for Jesus in everything you do so you will have maximum impact that will change the world of sports. It is time to get in the game!

Fifty-two devotions for athletes, coaches, and parents will transform the way you think. Each devotional features an in-the-trenches sports story with Scripture and life application, Be a GameChanger! section, room to write My Game Plan, and a heart and mind transforming prayer.

Book available at amazon.com, bn.com, and christianbook.com

Join the weekly WisdomWalks e-newsletter at www.wisdomwalks.org

---

Impacting the World for Christ through Sports

Fellowship of Christian Athletes is one of the world's largest sports ministry, reaching over two million people each year. Since 1954, FCA has cultivated Christian principles in local communities nationwide by encouraging, equipping, and empowering others to serve as examples and make a difference.

Fellowship of Christian Athletes | 8701 Leeds Road | Kansas City, MO 64129
www.fca.org • 800-289-0909

About the Authors

DAN BRITTON serves as the Fellowship of Christian Athletes' Executive Vice President of International Ministry. Dan played professional lacrosse for four years with the Baltimore Thunder, earning a spot on the All-Star team, and was nominated by his teammates for both the Service and Unsung Hero awards. Dan has coauthored four books, *One Word That Will Change Your Life*, *WisdomWalks*, *True Competitor*, and *Called To Greatness*, and he is the author and editor of twelve FCA books. He is a frequent speaker for companies, nonprofits, sports teams, schools, and churches. He still plays and coaches lacrosse and enjoys running and has competed in the Boston Marathon twice. He is married to Dawn, whom he met in youth group in eighth grade, and they reside in Overland Park, Kansas, with their three children: Kallie, Abby, and Elijah. You can e-mail Dan at dan@fca.org and follow him on Twitter @fcadan.

JIMMY PAGE serves as a Vice President of Field Ministry for the Fellowship of Christian Athletes. As a twenty-year leader in the health and fitness industry, he operated wellness facilities affiliated with Sinai Hospital and Johns Hopkins and now hosts a radio program called Fit Fridays. He and his wife, Ivelisse, started a cancer foundation called believebig.org following her victory over cancer. Jimmy has coauthored five books, *One Word That Will Change Your Life*, *WisdomWalks*, *PrayFit*, *True Competitor*, and *Called to Greatness*. He is a frequent speaker, challenging businesses, sports teams, schools, and ministries to maximize their potential and be their best. As a lifelong athlete, Jimmy still coaches, cycles, and competes in Spartan races and triathlons. Jimmy and Ivelisse are college sweethearts, residing in Maryland with their four children: Jimmy, Jacob, Johnny, and Gracie. You can email Jimmy at jpage@fca.org and follow him on Twitter @JimmyPageVT.

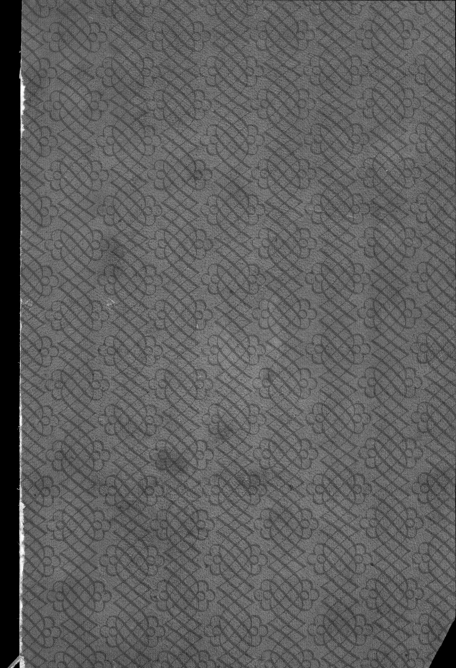

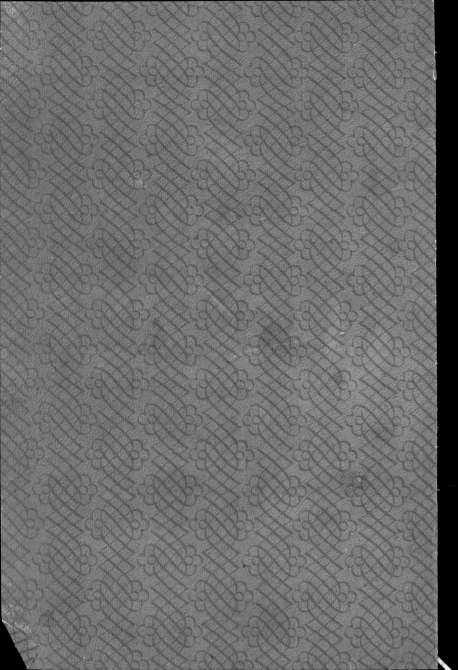